POSITIVE PASSIONATE PURPOSEFUL

IMPACTING LIVES THROUGH POSITIVITY AND ENCOURAGEMENT

A MOTIVATIONAL BOOK BY

LaShonda Pierce

PUBLISHED BY LAPIERCE PUBLISHING

POSITIVE PASSIONATE PURPOSEFUL

© 2019 by LaShonda Pierce

All rights reserved.

No portion of this book may be reproduced, stored in a retrieval system, or transmitted in any form or by means of electronic, mechanical, photocopy, recording, scanning, or another excerpt for brief quotations in critical reviews or articles, without the prior written permission of the publisher.

Published in Houston, Texas by
LaPierce Publishing

ISBN #978-0-692-18975-7 (paperback)
ISBN #978-0-692-18976-4 (ebook)

Edited By: Leah Pride

www.PositivePassionatePurposeful.com

PRINTED IN THE UNITED STATES OF AMERICA

TABLE OF CONTENTS

Dedication vii

Introduction... ix

The Power of Prayer...................................... 1

The Power in Positivity 25

The Power of a Positive Mindset 55

The Power of Addition............................. 83

The Power of Subtraction 111

The Power of Personal Peace................... 129

The Power of Faith Over Fear 141

The Power of Staying Positive
   (in spite of) 159

The Power of Positive Friends 173

The Power of Igniting Your Passion 195

The Power of Living Purposefully 209

Thank You... 239

"I WOULD RATHER BE ANNOYINGLY POSITIVE AND OPTIMISTIC, THAN DESTRUCTIVELY NEGATIVE AND HATEFUL."

~ Author Unknown

DEDICATION

This book is dedicated to my mother, Sonya Ann Pierce, for your love and great use of words. Although your dream of becoming an English teacher was interrupted by the life-changing tragedy that took precedence over your mind, I hope that my words can in some way reflect your unheard voice.

To my dear son, Keelyn, allow this book to be a symbolic token to never stop dreaming and working toward your dreams. I want to be living proof that dreams do come true.

INTRODUCTION

This book is more than empty motivation. It's filled with impactful substance, equipping you with knowledge to rejuvenate your spirit and realign your mindset. Each chapter was written to encourage the power of being positive, igniting your passion, in order to live purposefully. My hope is that the content of each page will inspire your life for the better. For the greatest impact, I suggest that you read this book in chronological order. Without question, the world we live in needs more love, common courtesy, and an understanding of the importance of making personal peace and prosperity, a priority. My desire is to inspire readers to take better care of their spirit, by silencing negativity and living PURPOSEFULLY.

I've managed to stay positive my entire life, regardless of what life has thrown my way. I've dealt with adversities that would make the average person ashamed, bitter, confused, socially awkward or mentally deflated. My life consists of being sexually abused (multiple times as a child), never knowing my father, and my mother being drugged by a so-called friend which made her mentally unstable and unable to raise her children.

My grandmother became a mother to my sister and brother, but unfortunately, she couldn't take on the responsibility of

Introduction

raising me at the time. As a result, I was separated from my immediate family at just two weeks old.

Although I endured years filled with hurt, unanswered questions, shame, and confusion, I'm forever grateful for God's hand over my life. I could have very well lost my mind, dignity, and self-worth; yet, through it all God's love was the glue that held my broken pieces together.

My nickname was "Peewee," which was quite fitting. I was a tiny little runt. Lord, I had little everything…little short nappy hair, little to no luxuries and apparently very little lotion because it seems I was always ashy. It's safe to say the struggle was real!

Let's be clear, I'm not asking for sympathy by mentioning these unfortunate things. The moral of the story is that although my life has been filled with pain and adversities, I am able to stand with my head held high and can proudly say I survived…

Today, I am a courageous, well-balanced woman, with the power to withstand any challenge. My heart overflows with an enormous amount of faith, love, and positivity that keeps me going. I didn't allow my circumstances to bury me in darkness, yet instead, be the fuel to shine the light over my life. I want people to know that if you stay positive, connected to God, and work hard you can overcome any challenge!

Many people expect writers to hold a certain level of "perfected credibility". I believe the wisdom gained from your life's lessons and how you handle them is what affords you the right to tell or write your story. No matter what life has thrown my way, I haven't given up. Hopefully, that reason alone will encourage someone to continue to pursue a more *positive*, *passionate* and *purposeful* life.

My purpose is bigger than my petite 5'2" frame. I proudly hold a Ph.D. in love and compassion, an accolade that the most prestigious schools can't teach.

I am walking in my purpose as an Interior and Fashion Designer of LaPierce Design, and a philanthropist through I.C.O.N. Women's Organization, a 501c3 nonprofit, of which I co-founded. This organization caters to educating and elevating women and youth in the greater Houston area. My life's mission is "Ensuring that People Look and Live Beautifully through Positivity, Fashion, and Interior Design." A collaboration of Life, Fashion & Interior Design;

POSITIVE · PASSIONATE · PURPOSEFUL

Ensuring A Lucrative Life, Effortless Style, and Spectacular Spaces. My passion ignites me to design beautiful spaces, clothing, and home accents daily. I desire to bring out the beauty in people, through encouraging and reminding men and women that a great future doesn't require a great past.

Through it all, we just have to keep praying, keep trying, keep smiling, and keep pressing forward IN SPITE OF… whatever life takes us through. Shout out to myself and anyone who still has love, light, and a heart of gold – remaining positive in spite of.

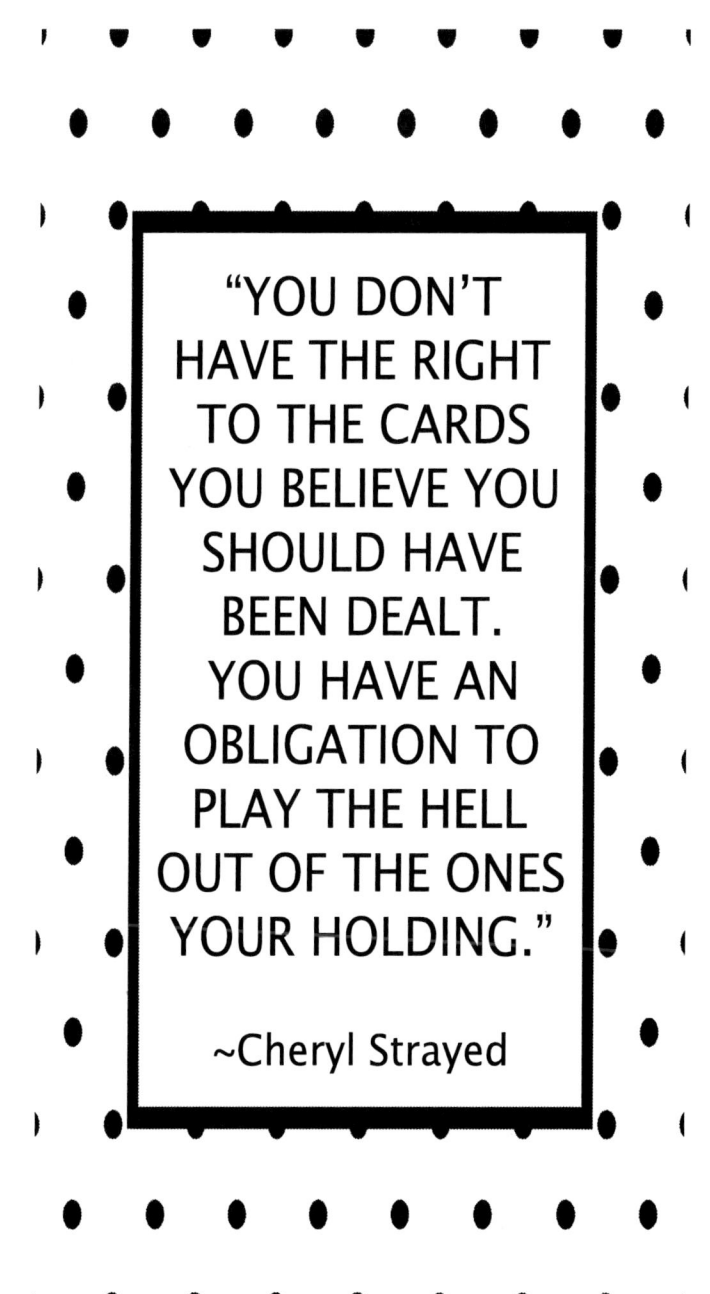

"YOU DON'T HAVE THE RIGHT TO THE CARDS YOU BELIEVE YOU SHOULD HAVE BEEN DEALT. YOU HAVE AN OBLIGATION TO PLAY THE HELL OUT OF THE ONES YOUR HOLDING."

~Cheryl Strayed

"PRAY, IT WORKS"

~ Author Unknown

CHAPTER 1

THE POWER OF PRAYER

First things first, I think it's important that you know God is the head and center of my life. Without Him, I am nothing. If you haven't done so already, I encourage you to invite Christ into your heart. I truly believe the key to securing a positive life is to include God in all you do. There is power in prayer and having a personal relationship with God.

Prayer is a mandatory component of living positively. God wants to be included in all that we do. He longs to order our steps and bring out the very best in each of us. With the power of God, no battle can defeat you, his power is within you. The only way this can occur is if we invite Him into every area of our lives.

What is prayer? It's a solemn request for help, an expression of thanks addressed to God or an object of worship.

Prayer is special and sacred and should be treated as if we're in the presence of God. Prayer softens the heart, eases the pain, and helps navigate your life to greatness. God's joy is refreshing. You don't have to be a saint, theological graduate, pastor, or mega-minister to pray, just a normal God-fearing human being.

If you are not Christian, please don't let this deter you from reading this book. Prayer is personal and can be applied to our lives individually. I can only share the greatness I've personally experienced with Christ. Connecting with God through prayer has gotten me through some of my most challenging days. For example, as a mother I've had to go heavily in prayer asking God to cover my child from the top of his head to the bottom of his feet. When I've felt alone, defeated, heartbroken and confused prayer has gotten me through.

Now, don't get it twisted. I'm no bishop or first lady that carries holy water in my purse. I don't talk in tongues nor have healing hands; however, I can navigate my way through the Bible and go to God in prayer during my most difficult moments. I simply want the same for you.

As a business owner, there are days I feel strong, talented, and powerful. There are also days I question myself and feel like giving up. Some days there's money in my account. Some days there isn't. Obviously, this can be very stressful. I work hard every day because I must. I wasn't born into luxury or generational wealth. I don't have handouts to rely on. I have a son, fiscal responsibilities, and business that I must handle. Therefore, it's a must that I pray daily for the strength to keep going.

I walk vigorously in the passionate pursuit of my purpose. I want you to understand I would not be able to navigate through life without connecting to God daily through prayer. I realize that even on my darkest days I'm still living my dream. I can recall praying and wishing for the very things I have today. I prayed for the opportunity to become a sought-after interior designer. I prayed for clients with beautiful spaces and the opportunity to spend every day doing what I love — utilizing my God-given talent and my prayers were answered. That's why even in times of difficulty, I'm reminded of God's faithfulness and that I'm still blessed.

I don't know it all, nor do I have it all figured out, but I do know that I'm absolutely nothing without God's daily mercy and grace. Prayer helps me in every aspect of my life. When I'm weary and confused, I pray. When I'm disappointed, I pray. When life is filled with celebratory moments, I continue to pray and give God praise. During good and bad times, I call on the name of Jesus to find peace, strength, and clarity. I encourage you to connect with God for perfect harmony and peace.

BECAUSE OF GOD, I AM:
FOUND.
BLESSED.
INSPIRED.
STRONGER.
SAVED.
HOPEFUL.
FORGIVEN.
AND LOVED.

PRAYING WITH CONFIDENCE

I believe in order to receive the victory of God's Blessings in your life; you must really understand the importance of praying correctly. Many people tend to pray a programmed, memorized, repetitious type of prayer, or perhaps the proper profound prayer mimicking deacon so and so, or only praying when in need. The truth is God wants us to have **bold authentic prayers**. He longs for you to simply be yourself and talk to Him as if he's your friend; you may as well, he knows everything about you anyway. You don't have to pray long to pray strong.

Simply go to God in prayer repenting and asking for forgiveness, because nine times out of ten, even though you're perfect, you've fallen short in achieving the high standards of his goodness.

I DON'T KNOW WHO NEEDS TO HEAR THIS BUT...

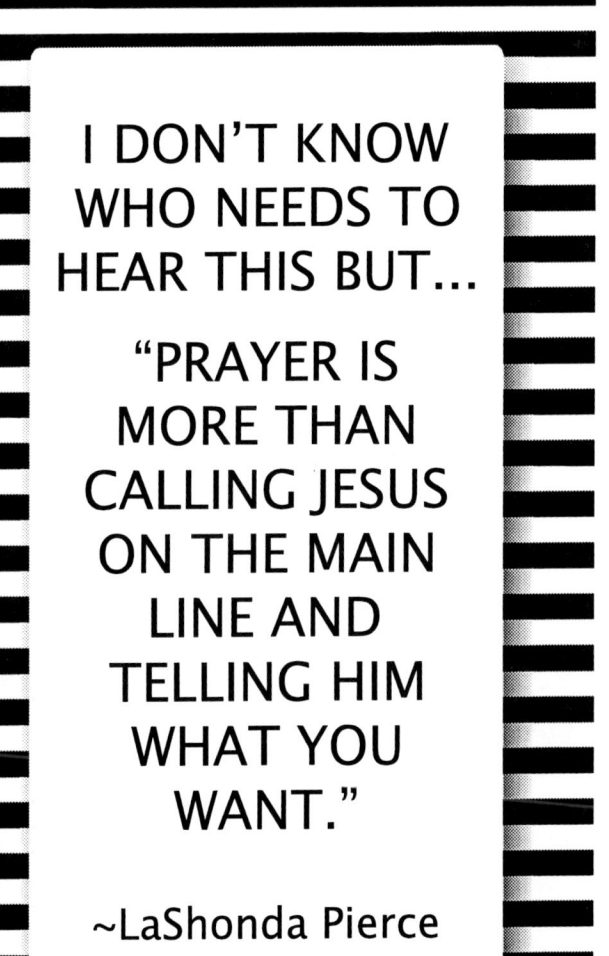

"PRAYER IS MORE THAN CALLING JESUS ON THE MAIN LINE AND TELLING HIM WHAT YOU WANT."

~LaShonda Pierce

Yes, God loves us and wants to abundantly bless us; however, he does expect us to live a life honoring Him and his commandments. That means, be mindful of the unlimited calls you make (telling Him what you want).

Here are a few vital steps to praying…

#1. Confess your sins and ask for forgiveness (remember you can't keep secrets from God) in order to be forgiven you must first confess your sins.

#2. Examine your relationship with God. We must live a life that's pleasing to God prior to sending up such GRAND REQUESTS to heaven. Trust me I know it's hard for many of us because we all fall short of God's glory. It's as if sin waits to greet us every day. If you're anything like me, then your spirit becomes convicted when the thought of sin arises because you know right from wrong. As hard as the temptation is, we must be mindful of sacred versus secular lifestyles and try extremely hard to live a life pleasing to God and not of the world. A great way to examine your relationship is to truly acknowledge the status with Him at your time of prayer.

How's your Christian behavior?

Come use your imagination with me...

Imagine being a child who has not had such a great week at school. You've acted out in every way possible; yet you have the audacity to ask your parents for a grand reward, all while knowing how they would respond to bad behavior. Crazy, right? You muscle up the courage to go to them anyway (like calling Jesus on the main line, telling Him what you want). Your parents scratch their heads in pure amazement because you really had the audacity to ask and they respond, "Why would I reward you when you haven't behaved correctly?" Ha-ha!

Much like our parents, God forgives and loves us unconditionally. However, we should still live life feeling convicted of sin and try to live a life pleasing to Him in order to go to Him confidently in prayer. God is always watching. The truth is many people (myself included) are half and half with God. Living half right! One foot in and one foot out.

For example:
† Married but not committed…
† Single but not celibate…
† Prosperous but not giving…

The Power of Prayer

The list goes on and on. The truth is we are selfish and want easy miracles from God but don't want to put in the work. A good friend of mine, Maven Miara Shaw, reminds her business clients, "The work is not skippable." I'm here to remind you that the work isn't skippable with God as well. We need to follow the commandments of God and do the work.

Another question to ask yourself is: How much time do you spend with God? Do you only pray when you need something or when times are tough? It's not fair to have a one-sided relationship; you've got to pray and give praise through the good and bad times. God loves when you can worship him in spite of what you're going through.

All relationships should be reciprocal, especially your relationship with God. Do you like to give, give, give, and never receive? Well, neither does The Most High. Are you living according to his will? Be honest with yourself and keep the answer in mind when going to prayer.

#3. Examine your relationship with family and loved ones. This one can be difficult. While everyone points the finger; especially because you're the only one in your family honest and with good sense, right? Ha-ha, go figure! All jokes aside, remember no one is perfect, not even you, my friend.

I have reason to believe that there are toxic traits within all of us that we must be honest about. Before kneeling to God in prayer we have to fix any relationship that's not of love and in order. Get any strife and conflict off your conscious. God is a loving God and wants peace. Remove any bitterness from your heart and walk in love. I've learned even when I feel wronged or there's any sort of strife with a loved one, to simply start with myself. Yes, that's right, start with yourself and ask God to work on you!

How does that sound?

Take a deep breath release the tension and repeat after me:

Lord renew a clean spirit within me.

Lord refresh my heart.

Lord cleanse my mind.

Lord free me from anger and tension. Forgive and teach me to walk in love like you.

In Jesus name,

Amen

You see, life is short. Love always wins and covers a multitude of sins, so even if you love friends or loved ones from a distance, don't forget that you too aren't spotless and need a soul cleansing as well.

#4. Examine your relationship with your church family. My pastor, Byron Stevenson, reminds us that a good standing member is more than someone that goes to church every Sunday, smiling and looking good. They are active and make sacrifices, like serving, giving support, lending a hand, and tithing.

All I'm suggesting is to be more than a pretty or handsome pew filler. Share your time, talents, and treasures with your church. This goes for me as well , as much as I love to smile and greet people I, too, should be actively serving in my church's greeting ministry.

I hope these suggestions make you feel more conscious about your relationship with God so that you can not only pray **_but pray with confidence._** We all are a work in progress, but if we act accordingly and follow his commandments, we can definitely be more confident in prayer. When we know better, we to do better.

There are so many more awaiting adventures and accomplishments I aspire to do in my lifetime. So every day I pray for God's direction to order my steps and give me the strength to remain positive, passionate, and purposeful.

Listed below are some go-to prayers and tips…

When You Are Stressed

Peace I leave with you; my peace I give you. I do not give to you as the world gives. Do not let your hearts be troubled and do not be afraid.

~ John 14:27

When You Are Happy

Rejoice always, pray continually, give thanks in all circumstances; for this is God's will for you in Christ Jesus.

~ 1 Thessalonians 5:16-18

When You Are Sad

He heals the brokenhearted and binds up their wounds.

~ Psalm 147:3

When You Are Anxious

Do not be anxious about anything, but in every situation, by prayer and petition, with thanksgiving, present your requests to God. And the peace of God, which transcends all understanding, will guard your hearts and your minds in Christ Jesus.

~ Philippians 4:6-7

When You Are Excited

May the God of hope fill you with all joy and peace as you trust in Him, so that you may overflow with hope by the power of the Holy Spirit.

~ Romans 15:13

When You Are Discouraged

Have I not commanded you? Be strong and courageous. Do not be afraid; do not be dis-

couraged, for the Lord your God will be with you wherever you go.

~ Joshua 1:9

When You Are Grieving
Blessed are those who mourn, for they will be comforted.

~ Matthew 5:4

When You Need Comfort
I have told you these things, so that in me you may have peace. In this world, you will have trouble. But take heart! I have overcome the world.

~ John 16:33

When You Are Scared
Be strong and courageous. Do not be afraid or terrified because of them, for the Lord

your God goes with you; he will never leave you nor forsake you.

~ Deuteronomy 31:16

WHEN YOU ARE INSECURE
For I know the plans I have for you," declares the Lord, "plans to prosper you and not to harm you, plans to give you h

~ Jeremiah 29:11

WHEN YOU ARE ANGRY
Create in me a clean heart, O GOD, AND renew a right spirit within me.

Psalm 51:10

A gentle answer turns away wrath, but a harsh word stirs up anger.

~ Proverbs 15:1

When You Are Lonely

Even though I walk through the darkest valley, I will fear no evil, for you are with me; your rod and your staff, they comfort me.

~ Psalm 23:4

Tips after you invite Christ into your life:
- Join a church in your community, be active, and attend regularly.
- Subscribe to daily devotional readings.
- Meditate or journal your thoughts and prayers.
- Repent, be honest and talk to God authentically.
- Examine your relationships and Christian behavior.
- Invite God into your daily affairs.

"LIFE IS FRAGILE, HANDLE IT WITH PRAYER."

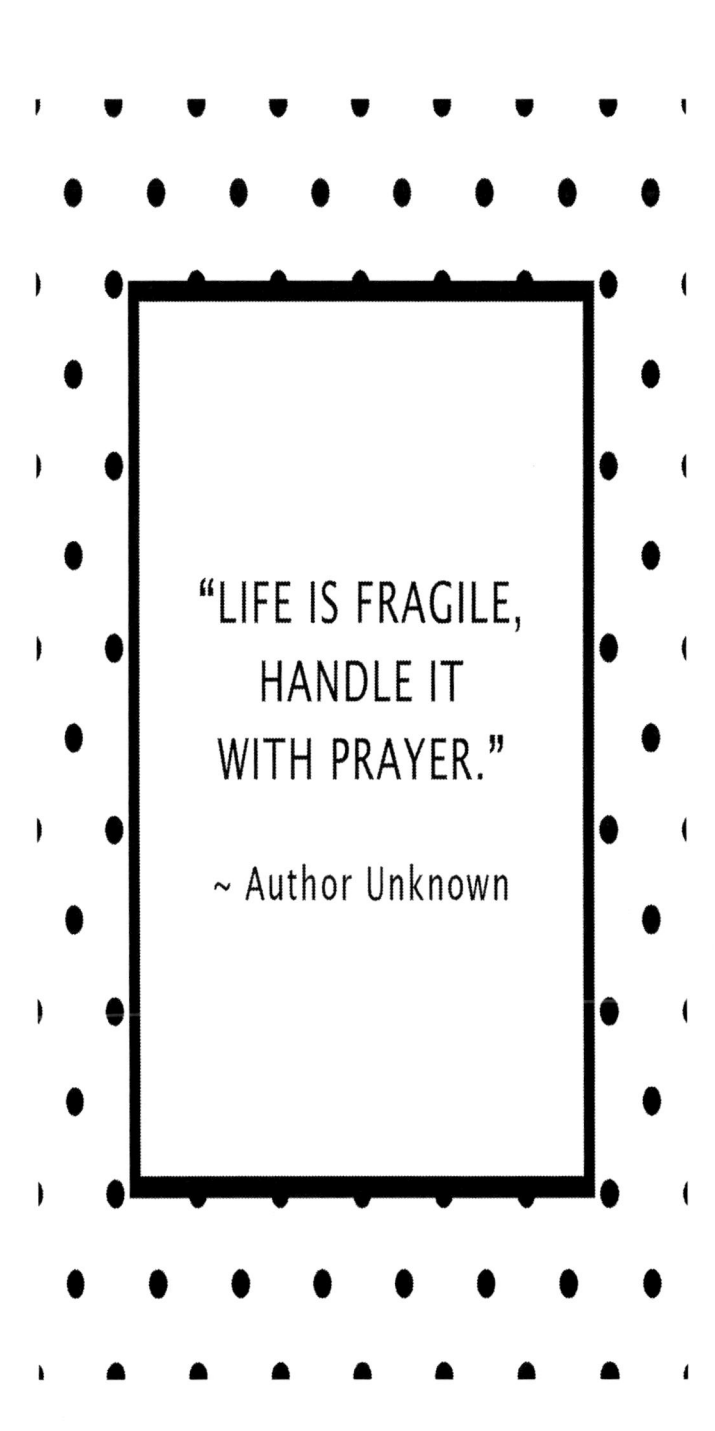

~ Author Unknown

CHAPTER 2

THE POWER OF POSITIVITY

SAY IT OUT LOUD!

P – POSITIVE

O – OUTLOOK

W – WHENEVER

E – EVIL

R – REVEALS ITSELF

P – POISED
O – OPTIMISTIC
S – STANCE
I – IN
T – TROUBLE
I – INDICATING
V – VICTORY
E – EVERY TIME

BE POSITIVE · STAY PASSIONATE · LIVE PURPOSEFULLY

POSITIVE · PASSIONATE · PURPOSEFUL

Repeat after me…
There's power in positivity!
Say it again…
There's power in positivity!

(You didn't think I had my megaphone on the cover of the book for nothing did you?)

Now, that we're fresh from the "Positive Pep Rally," let me warn you that this is the longest chapter in the book. Simply because it's such a major factor in living your best life. Keep your positive pants on and let's get POSITIVE!

There's power in positivity! Meaning, there's a positive outlook whenever evil reveals itself. **No matter what we are facing we must have the proper perspective and that is to always remain positive, having a poised optimistic stance in the time of trouble, indicating victory every time!**

I'm passionate about positivity because it's associated with love. God is love and God is positive. If we reflect Him, then we will live a life that demonstrates that same love and positivity. Unfortunately, the world we live in is filled with so much hate, hardened hearts, and negativity. Therefore, we need this pivotal chapter to help soften hearts, improve spirits and mentalities daily while spreading as much positivity as possible.

To live your best positive life, you truly must believe that *there is power in positivity!*

Positivity is a superpower! It is the power of always maintaining self control while holding on to your peace and maintaining freedom from disturbance, especially during difficult times that would seemingly steal your joy.

POSITIVE · PASSIONATE · PURPOSEFUL

It's easy to say the latest positivity quotes and have them written all over our t-shirts, bumper stickers, and social media timelines. However, just how many people are REALLY practicing positivity and enriching not only their lives but the lives of others?

Don't be the person pretending to be positive by posting a catchy heartwarming quote on social media but have an ice-cold heart in person.

I need you to really live a life with love and positivity in your actions and spirits. We all have enough battles in life to fight, so let's not make negativity another war. My goal is for the content of this book to inspire and equip readers with refreshing, positive outlooks worldwide I pray that through the prayers, messages, and journaling material offered within these pages, someone decides to end the warfare of negativity and implement daily positive habits toward living their best positive, passionate, and purposeful life!

So many people are after social status, job titles, and material wealth. In my opinion, the most desirable life quality is how we treat each other and to be filled with spiritual wealth. We need to be rich in spirit, rich in peace, and rich in positivity. There's power in possessing these fine qualities.

I'm wise enough to know that regardless of how attractive, smart, wealthy, or cool you "think" you are, ultimately your character and how you treat people is your true treasure of life. I can't help but wonder how wealthy many would be if our bank accounts were reflected by the way we treated one another.

"TOO OFTEN WE UNDERESTIMATE THE POWER OF A TOUCH, A KIND WORD, A LISTENING EAR, AN HONEST COMPLIMENT, OR THE SMALLEST ACT OF CARING, ALL OF WHICH HAVE THE POTENTIAL TO TURN A LIFE AROUND".

~ Leo Buscaglia

Just how appealing would you be based on the way you treat people, especially the ones you think you don't need? How attractive are your thoughts? There are so many ugly behaviors masked behind external beauty and material wealth that the world needs to stop glorifying.

I see some of the prettiest people with the ugliest behaviors. Looking down on people that they don't respect and feel aren't as good as them. I was taught to treat everyone the same.

Don't envy glitz, glam, money, fame, or titles. Instead, be impressed with and seek after the summation of love, kindness, compassion, integrity, and humility. It's the real new rich! Don't desire to be well known. Instead, strive to be worth knowing.

> *Finally, brothers, whatever is true, whatever is noble, whatever is right, whatever is pure, whatever is lovely, whatever is admirable — If anything is excellent and praiseworthy — think about such things.*
>
> ~ Philippians 4:8

So, here's the deal…

You can't have negative habits, be unkind, unpleasant, or unfriendly and expect to live a positive life that embodies the love of God. Living positively is a behavior. It's something you do every day. It's how you think. It's how you speak and how you interact. IT'S HOW YOU LOVE! We must make it a habit to do everything with so much love in our hearts that we feel convicted doing it any other way. I talked about the power of prayer in the first chapter, and I want to emphasize an important factor in the quote below.

"We can't pray in love and live in hate and still think we are worshiping God."

~ A.W. Tozer

When living a life of positivity, you can't straddle the fence of love and hate or indulge in both positive and negative behaviors. You can hide who you truly are from everyone except God. Be consistent with love, peace, kindness, and positivity. Be known for the way you treat people.

Living with love is a legacy I strive to be known for and it's my hope that others emulate this desire as well. The great thing about living a life of love is that it doesn't take money to leave this legacy. You simply invest with your heart. It costs absolutely nothing to be kind — not one red cent.

When living positively, it's important to live our best individual lives. However, it's also important to be cognizant of the impact our lives have on others. There's always someone watching and possibly admiring the way you live your life. Therefore, you should make it genuinely impactful and meaningful.

The way we live our lives can hurt or heal someone else. Are you hurting or healing? The positive impact of one human is a powerful inspiration. You can do simple things like spreading good energy, leading by an example of excellence, offering help, conveying knowledge, or showing kindness and support to impact someone else's life for the better.

"TRY TO BE A RAINBOW IN SOMEONE ELSE'S CLOUD."

~ Maya Angelou

Be intentional daily about how you can lend your hand and heart to help someone else.

Being positive is good for our health. It can lengthen our lives. Being positive is a pretty enhancement of life. You get an attractive glow and aura from spreading love, focusing on pursuing greatness, eliminating hate, and dismissing negativity.

Live BEAUTIFULLY! Be Positive!

I challenge both men and women to aspire to be more attractive by embracing an attractive heart, mind, and spirit. Let's not hide behind façades, masks, and faces full of makeup PRETENDING TO BE PRETTY with ugly insides.

I'm reminded of a car I once had; it was shiny and polished on the outside. However, its engine was bad. It looked pretty but it wasn't a pleasant ride. I can't help but think of many people like this — appearing pretty on the outside, but really internally damaged, calling everyone ugly but themselves.

Don't be shiny yet shallow.

~ LaShonda Pierce

As a personal stylist, I tell my clients I've got your outside covered. You'll be flawless and well put together. You just make sure your insides match your fly.

Once you start looking at people's hearts and spirits instead of glorified appearances, they begin to look different. Make people fall in love with your energy, personality, and heart. These qualities possess a beauty that doesn't age.

As beautiful as this is, I regret to inform you that although being positive is a lucrative way of life, everyone won't welcome your happy-go-lucky outlook. If that is the case, continue to love and give grace anyway. Learn to go where your energy is valued, matched, and commemorated. I've experienced people that have thought my positive behavior was an act or a facade or even a sign of weakness.

"Do they not know I'm Holy enough to pray yet hood enough to swing on you?!!"
(Lol just joking!)

In all seriousness, I've learned to remain true to myself. This means I've had to speak when I wasn't spoken to and show respect when it wasn't given to me. I've had to humble myself in order to honor myself by putting positivity over pettiness.

We must not treat people as bad as they are; instead, treat them as good as you are.

It's important to maintain a positive attitude if you want to experience a happier life. It's important to be optimistic and positive about everything you do and trust that things will manifest in your life. Being positive make souls more desirable to be around. People crave your presence and want to experience your good vibes and good energy. No one likes to be around Negative Nancy, Mad Michael, or Hateful Heather. Please don't let life change your name…

What's your Negative Nancy?

Is it hard for you to see the bright side of life? Is it hard for you to keep hope alive? Have you gone through a divorce? Do you desire to be more physically fit? Have you been incarcerated and find it hard to stay positive after being released from prison? Are you frequently unemployed? Are you struggling with substance abuse? Do you suffer from time management? Do you find yourself in conflict with negative people? Are you constantly robbing Peter to pay Paul? Do you suffer from anger issues? Have you given up on your dreams?

Whatever it is, let me remind you that no one is perfect; we all suffer from something.

Romans 3:23 says...

We have all sinned and fell short of the glory of God.

Power of Positivity

Pick your head up, remain positive, keep igniting your passions, and chasing your dreams to live purposefully. Don't let life get you down. Smile, your circumstances will change just stay positive and persistent.

Remember, if you can stay positive in a negative situation, you win. As far as remaining positive when dealing with negative people, just continue to love.

Moreover, it doesn't make you weak. It makes you strong. That's a super power! Ignore petty people PERIOD.

The phenomenal former FLOTUS, Michelle Obama, said it best during her Democratic National Convention speech: "When they go low, we go high." Those seven simple words resonated with my soul. We shouldn't lower our character by constantly getting down and dirty with people. Rise above pettiness and stay clear of senseless drama and negativity.

I often hear people say, "Everyone is just not warm and fuzzy nor nice and friendly." Yes, that's very true; I know that it does exist. However, I refuse to make excuses for rude people with character flaws and need to improve themselves. I've learned that people can be fickle — sometimes they're happy, sometimes they're dry, sometimes they speak, sometimes they won't, sometimes they love you other times they don't.

It's like, whew chile what are we doing today? One thing is for certain, the energy you feel doesn't lie. I want to encourage you, to respond right even if you feel wronged. The best response toward negative energy is to elevate higher and shine brighter!

We only have one life, so I suggest entertaining love, by putting positivity over pettiness. Don't hinder your blessings trying to treat people the way they treat you. Be kind anyway. If you return evil for evil, it makes you just as malicious as them. Compliment anyway. Show support anyway. Sow good seeds anyway. Allow love to win.

> *Do not repay evil with evil or insult with insult. On the contrary, repay evil with blessing, because to this you were called so that you may inherit a blessing.*
>
> *~ 1 Peter 3:9*

"YOU CAN'T CONTROL HOW OTHER PEOPLE RECEIVE YOUR ENERGY. ANYTHING YOU SAY OR DO GETS FILTERED THROUGH THE LENS OF WHATEVER PERSONAL STUFF THEY ARE GOING THROUGH AT THE MOMENT. WHICH IS NOT ABOUT YOU. JUST KEEP DOING YOUR THING WITH AS MUCH INTEGRITY AND LOVE AS POSSIBLE."

~Author Unknown

It's okay to be pleasant and to smile at frowns and unfamiliar faces. I do it every day. Initiating peace is powerful! We are all traveling on this journey of life, and kindness makes the voyage much more delightful. If we walk with the love of God in our hearts and positivity in our spirits, we will all reach our destination much more happily.

Make smiling a habit.
It's a gesture that welcomes peace.

~LaShonda Pierce

Living positively is being optimistic and looking on the bright side. I believe if positivity were a color, it would be bright yellow, like a ray of sunshine! Negativity is much too dark and gloomy.

Everyone knows that you can't live in the dark so keep the lights on in your life.

~ LaShonda Pierce

Light is always greater than darkness. You should constantly keep the light on in your life. In the words of Rihanna, "Shine bright like a diamond!"

Positivity is programming the mind to see the light in dark situations. Getting out of the tunnel of darkness (negativity) can save lives. Think of positivity as the light that paves the way. Be intentional about diminishing negativity and creating more positive experiences. I challenge you to rise above negative thinking and negative people. Make negative thinking a mindset of the past.

Positive thoughts help establish positive life experiences. Until we implement change in the way we think, we will block the possibilities of living a positive life. Keep your head up and tune out negativity. Join the positive party. Sing in the rain, dance through your storms, make lemonade from lemons, and build with bricks thrown at you. Just hold on to your power by ALWAYS STAYING POSITIVE!

WHAT IS THE TONE OF POSITIVITY?

When I think of living positively, I imagine living in perfect peace and perfect harmony. I imagine it to be a soothing and happy life experience while trusting that everything is going to work out for the highest good. I envision uninterrupted tranquility and warmth.

Now, don't get me wrong, I'm not living in a bubble in a magical unicorn world. I'm aware that for most people staying positive in a negative situation is difficult. There are countless "daily disturbances" and life experiences that can easily shift your energy from positive to negative. However, you must learn to accept situations and maintain your peace. I know that every day will not be a good day, but we should show up optimistic and do so without a second thought.

During my difficult moments I, too, must practice what I preach. I've dealt with many uncomfortable moments — past due bills, a broken heart, empty bank accounts and what seems to be more valleys than peaks. I've had to have several pep talks reminding myself to **be positive,**

stay passionate, and live purposefully. That applies to all of us. Life gets real and I'm not excluded. I've had to pray and pep talk my way through many days.

For instance, I've had to close my eyes and pray prior to checking my account balance, because Lord knows I don't need any negativity in my life. (lol) No, seriously, I've driven to work with tears running down my face and have had to pull myself together before knocking on a client's door.

I have had to put my problems aside and put my game face on so that I can fulfill my purpose. Yes, I know being positive 24/7 is not an easy task but it's certainly necessary. I encourage you to call on the name of Jesus when you find it hard to remain positive. He'll help you get through. Being a positive person doesn't protect you from the inevitable, natural, or emotional storms of life. However, God loves when we can praise Him during the storm.

To live positively, we must tune out negativity and keep our hopes, energy, and emotional state high at all times. We must learn to ignore anyone or anything that can get us out of character by being disciplined about what we react to and how we respond.

Tenderize your heart, and don't let the world take you from warm to cold or shift your energy from sweet to sour. Instead, delight in the atmosphere of love. Learn to pause and pray before you allow negativity to have its way.

THEY SAY YOU ARE WHAT YOU EAT...

I love the phrase: "Eat diamonds for breakfast and shine all day." The truth is, we must get in the habit of eating diamonds for breakfast so that we can literally shine all day. Eating diamonds refers to feeding your mind, body, and soul with the daily nutrients of positive thoughts and good energy. We must feed our minds positive thoughts. The recipe of peace and positivity is to feed your soul the best ingredients of life.

Get full on faith, hope, kindness, empathy, compassion, love, generosity, grace, peacefulness, enthusiasm, respectfulness, sincerity, politeness, thoughtfulness, gentleness, friendliness, selflessness, and more.

Forgive me for the comparison, but please hear me out. I can't help but think about when we are sick and have to vomit. Whatever is in our body at that time comes up and out. That's much like whatever is in our hearts, spirits, and minds comes out of our mouths, in our actions, and shows in our demeanor. I don't know anyone that likes to be sick or vomit, as it's usually foul and unpleasant based on what we've eaten.

I challenge you to be mindful about what you feed yourselves spiritually. We have all heard the phrase, "We are what we eat!" It's such a true statement. We truly are what's inside of us. Watch your diet, detox your mind and body of negativity! Be mindful of the ugly that goes in… as it comes out in one way or the other.

> *And he says what comes out of a person is what defiles him. For from within, out of the heart of man, come evil thoughts, wickedness, deceit, sensuality, envy, slander, pride, foolishness. All*

of these evil things come from within and they defile a person.

~ Mark 7:20-23

Positivity is so important because it is a direct reflection of who you are and what's in your heart. Be careful of what's put into the universe. There's power in thoughts and the tongue. Exterior beauty is okay, but beautiful insides are sensational! Keep your heart beautiful; don't litter your body with negativity. Live with love and pour beauty into the universe, one word and one measure at a time. Your actions determine how positive and beautiful you truly are.

Be Encouraged Friends, Live Beautifully!

CHAPTER 3

THE POWER OF A POSITIVE MIND SET

Mindset is what separates the best from the rest…

~Author unknown

Living positively is a mindset that we must put forth daily. The truth is if you change your mindset you will change your life. **There's magic in your mindset.** Reset your mindset — out with the old, in with the new. You must win in your mind in order to win in your life. Forgive me, but I love music and will make several references to songs, lyrics, and artist throughout the book. I can't help but think of when a sound engineer says "mic check, mic check" — every day we need a mind check, mind check!!

Our minds are trained to believe everything we tell it. Ultimately, what you tell yourself is what will manifest in your life. Therefore, we should saturate our minds with the word of God and positive thoughts. God is a positive God. He loves us unconditionally, forgives us of our sins, and consistently gives us daily mercy and grace. He renews, restores, and rebuilds us each day. God is optimistic and wants the best for our lives.

It's imperative that we take care of our mental wellness and mindsets. We are in charge of our minds from the moment we arise each morning! Positivity is a choice. Our days are established by how we spend the first moments of the day. Spend the first hour of your day doing things that add meaning and value to your life, like reading affirmations, praying, and thinking positive.

Sit still for a moment. Stillness is a way to take time out for you. We are all busy, but we should try to give ourselves at least five minutes of stillness, by learning to take deep breaths and exhaling. In other words, calm down! Relax your thoughts and racing heart. I've had to learn to settle my mind in the morning by closing all of the tabs racing in my head.

From the moment I wake up, I'm usually thinking of the task ahead instead of being gentle with myself by closing my cell phone, unplugging for a moment, and simply relaxing. Embrace the quietness of mental clarity. Don't allow your mind to work frantically. Your mindset ultimately determines the balance of your day. Just like there is power in the tongue, there is power in what we think; therefore, we must take control of the thoughts racing in our mind.

Own your day; don't let your day own you. What we think is what we get. And there is power in positive thinking! We must choose to be happy by thinking happy thoughts. Furthermore, we must speak, think, and believe that amazing opportunities are headed our way.

"Create the highest grandest vision possible for your life. Because you become what you believe."

~Oprah Winfrey

We live in a time where we can't afford to overlook mental health. Mindset and mental health go hand in hand. It should instead become a priority. Mental health has a lot to do with living positively. Our mind is a major component in the way we think and feel. So, we must not let negative thinking overwhelm and destroy us.

In recent times, we've witnessed the dark side of mental health with a vast number of suicides. Just what caused such amazing, talented, and remarkable individuals to end their lives? I believe the answer was darkness — the darkness of defeat, the darkness of loneliness, the darkness of difficulty, the darkness of debt, and the darkness of hopelessness. I believe darkness was what they thought about themselves, their lives, their future, and the situation they were facing. They couldn't see in the dark, nor could they see a way out of the darkness. **#depressionisraf**

I'd be lying if I said I've never been in a dark place and wondering if the world would be better without me. It's a heavy feeling. It's like being buried alive and trying to breathe while covered in darkness. The devil likes for us to feel as if hell is our final destiny. Without question, prayer saved my soul. I turned on the light in my life, thought about my son, my future grandchildren, and all of my unfinished work here on earth. God isn't finished with me yet nor is he finished with you.

We must learn to defeat depression by shining the bright yellow light over our lives and the lives of others. Break the habit of living in darkness and sorrow, speaking of your problems, and being hard on yourself and others. You should instead give praise and focus on the joys. You can be livid at life, people, and circumstances, or you can strive for greatness daily. Each day is a new beginning filled with new starts, new intentions, and new results.

I'm a morning person and love to open the blinds each day to allow the sunlight to shine in. I suggest that you, too, wake up every day and allow the sun to shine light in your life by finding simple reasons to smile and realize how blessed you are.

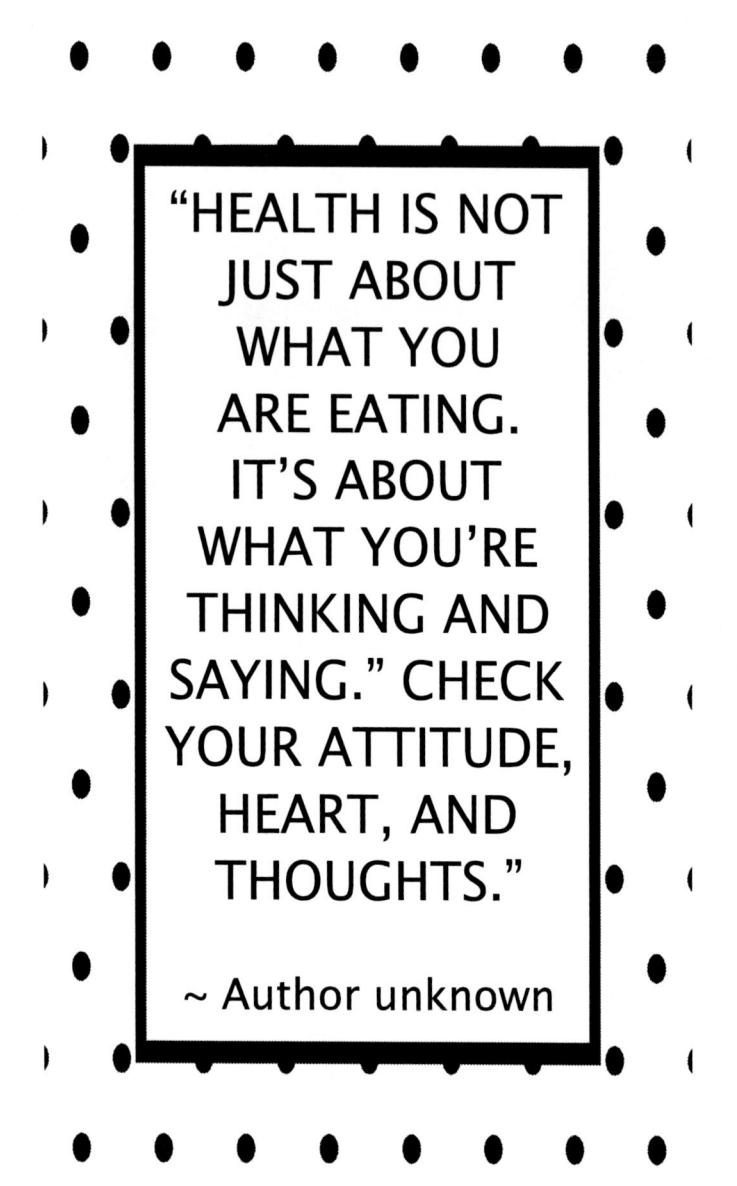

"HEALTH IS NOT JUST ABOUT WHAT YOU ARE EATING. IT'S ABOUT WHAT YOU'RE THINKING AND SAYING." CHECK YOUR ATTITUDE, HEART, AND THOUGHTS."

~ Author unknown

The Power of a Positive Mindset

There are so many things to be grateful for like: health, family, friends, freedom, food, shelter, transportation, a sweet dessert! It's imperative to feed your mind with positivity, peace, and love and learn to take inventory over your life and be thankful for the simple things.

The truth is, in life, we all get empty from time to time and need refueling. I fell in love with the words of Chance the Rapper while he was accepting an award. During his acceptance speech, he pleaded with the audience saying, "Gas me up!"

He, the talented multimillionaire, requested praise and applause. Why? He'd already won the award. Why was he requiring more validation? He asked because even with millions of dollars, a wall full of Grammy's, degrees, a garage full of cars, and bank accounts full of money, we are still humans with real souls and real heartbeats.

The truth is sometimes we need to be gassed up, refueled, cheered, and applauded! Not celebrating the victory of your fellow human is like going to a basketball game and not clapping for a winning shot, it's like not laughing at a comedy show, it's like not singing along during praise and worship at church! Although we can clap for ourselves, we still need to feel the love by connecting and sharing good energy amongst each other through encouragement.

"How you make others feel about themselves, says a lot about you".

~Author unknown

What I know for sure is…

- Everyone has a purpose.
- Everybody needs encouragement.
- Everybody has something unique to offer.
- God uses people to help people.

If you can't find anything good to say about others, then shame on you. Open your eyes and your heart and learn to share and spread love. I promise its okay to toot someone else's horn. It won't take anything from you if you show love to someone else. Everyone has something unique and great that's identifiable to others. I'm begging you to gas people up, see, cheer and encourage their potential. Fill up their tank by applauding their talents, great works, efforts, and treasures.

> *Stop the hate, congratulate,*
> *in return you elevate!*
>
> ~LaShonda Pierce

I'm too great for any form of hate. #inreallife

That's why I'm friendly, that's why I smile, that's why I congratulate and never hate, that why I can complement and double tap pictures immediately, that's why I cheer and encourage others to shine bright like a diamond. The light is within, be love and light.

Just as cars need full tanks of gas to take us from one place to another, so does your fellow human. I think it's sad when people are too selfish and self-centered to give someone else a compliment.

God's greatest command was for us to love Him and each other.
~ Matthew 22:36-40

You also need to learn to gas yourself up. The way you speak to yourself matters most, so build yourself up, compliment and love yourself without apologizing for it. I challenge you to take a long look in the mirror, take charge of your thoughts words, and intentions. Look past your faults and perceived imperfections and recognize the good and beautiful characteristics and traits within yourself. My advice would be to compliment yourself often and love yourself more than you expect anyone else to. Once you remind yourself of your greatness, you won't have to depend on others.

We often get so caught up on what we are not, the things that we want and are working towards, that we forget to highlight our gifts and recognize the daily mercy and grace God continuously gives. Social media has everyone appearing so perfect that we tend to be way too hard on ourselves. Some people think every post has to be perfect, or that you have to appear rich, smart, and flawless. Trust me no one has it all together the way it's strategically timed and displayed on IG. The moment we start giving ourselves more credit for how hard we are working and just how far we've come, we'll realize how richly blessed our lives are. It will then feel like the blessing it is.

Lives will never evolve until we implement change to our daily habits. The secret to successfully maintaining a positive mindset is by what we think and do daily. It's how we speak and the way we live, interact, and operate every day. We are what we constantly think; therefore, we must pray that God will continually strengthen our thoughts and minds. Focus on the positive! Learn to focus on the feel-goods for our energy goes where our attention is. SHIFT your thoughts to the positive.

It's easy to get distracted by the uncertainties and circumstances of life. That includes catastrophic events like divorce, bad decisions, failing health, career changes, financial challenges, failed friendships, family feuds, or any other example of life storms and troubling times. We still must fight to smile through the pain, laugh at the confusion, focus on the good, and realize that situations could always be worse.

I'M NO METEOROLOGIST BUT STAYING POSITIVE THROUGH CLOUDY DAYS IS A MINDSET THAT WILL HELP YOUR EYES STAY DRY DURING THE STORM.

~ LaShonda Pierce

The Power of a Positive Mindset

I've learned that everything happens for a reason. An occasional bad experience will help you learn to appreciate good experiences. I wasn't able to grow and develop a better mindset until I removed any trace of negative thinking from my thoughts. Whenever I find myself drifting into darkness, I immediately reprogram my thoughts. Negativity is way too heavy and can weigh down the mind, dampen your spirits, and ultimately subtract from your life.

Living in Houston during the crisis of Hurricane Harvey was life-changing for our city and state. Thousands of people were directly affected by the distress and devastation of the storm. Many homes were uprooted. Families were uncomfortable, inconvenienced, and displaced.

Yet, so many people in Texas and worldwide were neighborly and remained positive and focused on the good. Everyone put joy over circumstance. Witnessing civilians come together giving an outpour of love, support, and helping hands was so inspiring and a true definition of humanity and God's love. That's a perfect example of thinking and living positively during a storm of life.

There was a difficult time in my life when it felt like everything was falling apart. It became a struggle for me to be positive, stay passionate and live life purposefully. I was facing several challenges. I had eviction letters, little hope, and frankly no appetite to excel. I had a heart full of dreams but no fuel to mash the gas. I was on E; I was empty, depleted, exhausted, hopeless, and letting all my genius sink instead of soar. I simply wanted to give up and sleep the pain away.

I can recall going to one of my workrooms and one of my contractors asking me why I looked so down in the dumps. He went on to tell me that looking like what I was going through wasn't going to help the situation.

Furthermore, it wasn't easy on the eye. Instead, it only made the situation worse! I was spending too much time in a dark place, forgetting to honor the light within myself. I was kicking myself while I was down. His comments made a huge impact on me.

With my love and background in fashion and design, I know that when we look good, we feel good. Yet here I was looking like life had defeated me. After leaving the workroom that day, I took a long look in the mirror and had a "Coming to Jesus" moment. Somehow I forgot that I was "Fierce LaPierce", a fearless child of God! That day, I closed the chapter of hurt and regained my confidence and strength through prayer, positivity, some much-needed makeup, and upbeat music. I've learned that when you're down in the dumps, it's not the best time to look a mess and listen to sad music! Riding around listening to sorrowful music can only make it worse my friends. It's like being your own personal DJ at a pity party. Instead, you need to elevate your spirits higher when you are feeling low. Pump up the volume, the beat, and the tempo of your life. It's a vibe honey, get in tune with higher vibration and apply pressure! Apply pressure to what? Your dreams, your passions and the promises of God. I admire musicians, as music has healing power and connects with your soul.

One thing I know for sure is that sadness and depression can put you in a fetal position, causing you to become weak, vulnerable, and fragile. Those feelings are unhealthy. Dismiss depression through prayer, good music, and positivity. We need to be mad, not sad at the circumstances we encounter. A fighting mad attitude gives us the ammunition and grit we need to defeat the challenge. Every day you should wake, pray, and slay! Regardless of what you're faced with, never look like what you're going through. I often say many of us are photogenic, but life isn't picture perfect.

Yes, I take decent pictures with big bright smiles, in spite of whatever I may be going through, so it may appear as though I don't deal with the storms of life.

As a result, I recently received a message, "Can't nobody be that happy." That message really tickled me, as far as my happy face, Lil Wayne says it best...

> *"I can be flat broke and keep a million-dollar smile."*
>
> ~ Lil Wayne

I honestly prefer smiling rather than frowning. Many of us are photogenic but life is not picture perfect. I just chose happy in spite of. Yes, sometimes I smile when I really want to cry and keep going, when I really want to give up. I am often nice when people are mean. I help others when I need

The Power of a Positive Mindset

help myself. I show love to people who don't give it in return. Simply because that's what's inside of me. I don't let people or situations stop me from being *positive, passionate and purposeful*. Genuine love resides in me and my light shines through.

The truth is prayer, lyrics, and lipstick have helped me many days. This simple pick-me-up helps seize and conquer the day. Men don't typically wear makeup, but can still wake, worship, and win! The main objective is just not to stay down and rise above feeling low.

Most of our challenges have something to do with a lack — lack of hope, lack of health, lack love, or lack of finances. Just know we don't have to look like what we're going through; smile anyway! Sometimes we just have to pop our collars, and give ourselves a pep talk like: "Hey, I will not be defeated! I AM POSITIVE! I AM PASSIONATE! I AM PURPOSEFUL!

We can't waste valuable days crying and complaining. There's limited time for that and they don't serve champagne at pity parties, so I'm definitely not going! Demand the day by encouraging and trusting yourself and God while simply doing what you can. Whether male or female, remind yourself that you are a child of God and a beautiful masterpiece that can conquer all challenges.

> *I can do all things through Christ who strengthens me!*
>
> ~ Philippians 4:13

The Power of a Positive Mindset

Below are some things you can do to maintain a positive mindset:
- Pray
- Be positive
- Seek professional counseling
- Encourage yourself
- Journal
- Dance
- Work out
- Box
- Look your best
- Lift your chin up
- Stick your chest out
- Smile more
- Listen to happy music
- Be around happy people
- Be thankful
- Try harder
- Do what you can!

POSITIVE · PASSIONATE · PURPOSEFUL

ASK YOURSELF THE FOLLOWING QUESTIONS:

What negative thoughts and habits do I need to eliminate from my life?

_____

_____

_____

What are some positive things I can do at the start of the day?

_____

_____

What can I do when darkness arrives in my life?

_____

_____

_____

The Power of a Positive Mindset

In what ways can I leave a positive impact on others?

_____

_____

Gas yourself up. List all the positive traits about yourself. (Remind yourself of these daily by printing and framing.)

_____

_____

_____

_____

_____

_____

_____

_____

_____

BE POSITIVE · STAY PASSIONATE · LIVE PURPOSEFULLY

I CHANGED MY MINDSET
& CHANGED
MY LIFE"

~ Author Unknown

CHAPTER 4

THE POWER OF ADDITION

The 5 Key Ingredients to Adding Positive Energy to Your Life

To add is a bonus and being positive is a plus. It's important because it adds value to your life and to others. The people, places, and experiences we have should be adding to our lives not taking away. Much like baking a cake, there are key ingredients like flour, sugar, butter, eggs, and water that assures it will be delicious. Then there is that little extra something, something grandma adds to the cake

POSITIVE · PASSIONATE · PURPOSEFUL

to give it that extra kick of flavor. The same is true with positivity; there are a few key ingredients that you can add to your life that will increase your positivity!

Here are some essential things to add to your life:

Add Love

I associate positivity with love. Love is a key ingredient to living a life of peace and positivity. God is love. He is a positive God. Love is a beautiful attribute to life. Do all things with love.

> *Love is patient, love is kind. It does not envy. It does not boast. It is not proud. It does not dishonor others. It is not self-seeking. It is not easily angered. It keeps no record of wrongs.*

The Power of Addition

Love does not delight in evil but rejoices with the truth. It always protects, always trusts, always hopes, always perseveres. Love never fails.

~ 1 Corinthians 13:4-8

Life should be lived with love, compassion, and kindness. God loves a cheerful giver. People should feel the impact of love you've shared in whatever you do regardless of how large or small the act is.

I can recall facilitating a pop-up shop with I.C.O.N.'s Women's Organization. My team and I created a boutique-style shopping experience of donated clothing at one of Houston's largest shelters, The Star of Hope. Although the clothing was donated, everything we accepted and donated was in impeccable condition. We didn't give those women anything that we wouldn't want ourselves. The clothing was displayed on hangers and stylishly coordinated down to the accessories. We set everything up just like a high-end boutique with shopping bags and great customer service. We wanted the ladies who were already going through a lot to feel the LOVE in what we were doing and giving. And guess what, they did!

That's just one of many gratifying experiences the ladies of I.C.O.N. and I have done to serve those in need. We make sure everything we do for others in the community is done with empathy, excellence and sealed with lots of love. Learn how to show and give love to others and make their life experiences better. When you do something for someone, simply practice empathy by putting yourself in their shoes. Humble your heart and realize how it would feel if the shoe was on the other foot and you were in need.

I often joke with my young adult son. He hates taking pictures and he's also not very fond of being my personal photographer. "Take my picture with love so it will come out right!" I yell. Or perhaps when I make a delicious Sunday dinner, his response is, "Mom, I see you cooked with love today!" The moral of the story is people can feel your energy in everything you do, so do all things with love.

If you're a doctor, care for your patients with love. If you're a hairstylist, do hair with love. If you're a Realtor, sell homes with love. If you're a teacher, educate your students with love. If you're a CEO lead with love. Doing someone a favor? Do it with love. No matter if the act is big or small; just do all things with love. Love is a beautiful way of life. Let the people in your life know you love, value, and appreciate them.

The Power of Addition

ASK YOURSELF THE FOLLOWING QUESTIONS:

In what ways can you add love to your daily interactions?

_____

_____

_____

How can you spread love by helping others?

_____

_____

_____

How has the love you've given impacted others?

_____

_____

_____

BE POSITIVE · STAY PASSIONATE · LIVE PURPOSEFULLY

Add The Word of God

I personally want to thank my dear Aunt Pat for keeping my family connected to the word of God. We grew up in a small congregation by the name of Mt. Carmel Baptist Church on the south side of Houston, Texas throughout my childhood and young adult life. The biblical teachings I learned as a child, have stuck with me throughout my life. It seemed as if I was in church 24/7 growing up. We attended Sunday school, vacation Bible school, the church choir, drill team, mission programs, and more. It was frustrating as a kid but now, I'm appreciative for those experiences. God's word was planted in me and has become the foundation of my life.

I believe God's word is a vital positive weapon to negative warfare. There are cer-

The Power of Addition

tain scriptures I use frequently that help me battle negative circumstances in life. I call them my "Survival Scriptures." This is a way to take the word with you throughout your day.

I suggest keeping some go-to scriptures handy for your life by familiarizing yourself with scriptures that are relatable to you. File them in your memory, store them in your heart, or write them in your journal. Do whatever works for you; just keep them close for your time of need.

I recently got my first and only tattoo a few years ago. It's a Bible verse that's symbolic and meaningful to me. The tiny tattoo is tucked behind my left wrist reads…

~ Psalms 46:5

God is within her she will not fail.

It's my personal "Survival Scripture". It serves as a constant reminder that God is with me; therefore, I will not fail. Even on my lowest days, I gain a sense of hope and encouragement through this simple scripture. The verse reminds me not to give up and to keep pressing forward. I'm not suggesting you run out and get a tattoo. However, I am encouraging you to keep meaningful scriptures close to your heart and at your disposal.

When I was growing up, my grandmother, Alice, demanded that my cousins and I recite Bible verses before we could indulge in any meal. Of course we despised this because we were greedy little rug rats. We would try to be the first to claim the easy two-word verse known as, "Jesus wept," so we could have first dibs at the food. What I now realize is that my beloved grandmother was preparing us to familiarize ourselves with calling on the name of Jesus with brief but bountiful scriptures that could help save the day. This childhood ritual has blessed my adult life. We must re-energize our prayer life and learn to encourage ourselves through positive thinking and prayer daily:

The following are some of my favorite scriptures:

> *I can do all things through Christ who strengthens me.*
>
> ~ Philippians 4:13

> *In the morning Lord you hear my voice; in the morning I lay my requests before you and wait.*
>
> ~ Psalms 5:3

For I know the plans I have for you declares the Lord, plans to prosper you and not to harm you, plans to give you hope and a future.

~ Jeremiah 29:11

Jesus Christ is the same, yesterday, today and forever.

~Hebrews 13:8

Blessed are the pure of heart for they shall see God.

~ Matthew 5:8

The Lord is my light and my salvation; whom shall, I fear? The Lord is the strength of my life; of whom shall I be afraid?

~ Psalms 27

Love is patient, love is kind, it does not envy, it does not boast, it is not proud. It does not dishonor others, it is not self-seeking.
~ 1 Corinthians 13:4-7

Create in me a clean heart, O God; and renew a right spirit within me.
~ Psalms 51:10

And we know that all things work together for the good to those who are called according to His purpose.
~Romans 8:28

Trust in the Lord with all of your heart, and lean not on your own understanding; in all your ways acknowledge Him and He shall direct thy paths
~Proverbs 3; 5-6

POSITIVE · PASSIONATE · PURPOSEFUL

Ask yourself the following questions:

What are my go-to prayers and Bible verses?

_____

_____

What bible scriptures have lifted your spirit?

_____

_____

In what ways can I encourage myself?

_____

_____

_____

How can I encourage others?

_____

_____

_____

ADD JOY

Joy is the feeling of great pleasure and happiness. I want to live life being jovial, full of cheer, with lots of laughs, and good spirits. Laughter is one heck of a medicine and quite the pain killer. I absolutely love to laugh and try to giggle every chance I get. In fact, I'm often told I should quit my day job and become a comedian. I honestly don't try to be funny. I just naturally find the humor in most situations.

I encourage you to loosen up, go with the flow of life and seek the same. Never take the privilege of life's simple joys for granted. Don't dare waste precious joy living down in the dumps with worry and dreariness. We must not let situations, people, or things defeat our joy!

Joy is a decision, a really brave one, about how you are going to respond to life.

~ Wess Stafford

We must connect with joy, as we need this pivotal ingredient daily. We also must be cognizant of what takes our joy away and avoid it. If you can't seem to find the joy in your life, rejoice in the Lord. Go to God in intimate prayer for He can revitalize and rejuvenate your spirit.

Finding daily pleasure will lead to daily happiness and joy. We should have so much joy in our mannerism that we can rejoice through any situation. Look around you and take inventory. Find joy in the simple things surrounding your life. Rejoice in the Lord, find joy in your children, family, and friends. You can even find joy in your talent, hobbies, uniqueness, dreams, and desires of your heart. Simply find joy in Life! It's all around you!

> *May the God of hope fill you with all joy and peace as you trust in Him, so that you may overflow with hope by the power of the Holy Spirit.*
>
> ~ Romans 15:13

POSITIVE · PASSIONATE · PURPOSEFUL

Use the space below to list all the things that bring you joy:

_____

_____

_____

_____

_____

_____

_____

_____

_____

_____

_____

_____

_____

_____

_____

_____

ADD A SMILE

A smile is a pleasant facial expression, and the best unisex accessory ANYONE can wear. This is one of my favorite life ingredients! When I think of my best physical feature, it has to be my smile. It's my signature accessory and what I'm known for. I flash this thing every chance I get. You'd swear that my teeth were bright white or someone was telling me to say cheese! I can't explain it; it's just what I do. It's an inexpensive piece of wealth I love to share with others.

> *"A smile is a curve that sets everything straight."*
>
> ~ Phyllis Diller

So many people underestimate the power of a smile; it truly has the power to turn someone's day around.

> *"Make smiling a habit, it's a gesture that welcomes peace."*
>
> ~ LaShonda Pierce

Every human on this earth has a smile; it's a universal language. I challenge you to use and flash yours every chance you get. I believe adding the accessory of a smile will enhance your life and the lives of those around you. Smiling can navigate vibes and turn a dreary day and most situations into happier moments.

Smiles soften the atmosphere. The truth is, frowns are unattractive and unappealing. I realize that most individuals can't smile the entire twenty-four hours of the day. However, I do challenge you to at least aim for twenty-three and a half.

The Power of Addition

Smiles ignite a certain level of love and happiness. Be intentional about smiling. Exercise your cheeks. Smile more!

Take a moment and think about the last time you smiled…

POSITIVE · PASSIONATE · PURPOSEFUL

Ask yourself the following questions:

What activities make me smile?

_____

_____

_____

Who makes me smile?

_____

_____

_____

How often do I smile?

_____

_____

The Power of Addition

I smile the most when…

_____

_____

_____

_____

_____

_____

_____

_____

_____

_____

_____

_____

(Be mindful of the answers you provided above, and stay connected to those people, places, and things.)

ADD GRATITUDE

Gratitude is the quality of being thankful. It's the readiness to show appreciation for and to return kindness. If we could just learn to be ridiculously, off the chain, obsessively grateful and master being thankful for what we have, we'd realize just how rich we truly are. Practicing gratitude every day will naturally cause you to look for the good in people and experiences daily.

Break the chain of talking about the burdens and begin to talk about the blessings. Gratitude changes everything. It opens our eyes to the simple gifts all around us. Every morning while enjoying a hot shower, I close my eyes and begin to thank God for the simple blessings all around me. He's a good God and so worthy to be praised!

The Power of Addition

Most people sing in the shower, but I count my blessings, shout, and give God praise!

"Gratitude is the healthiest of all human emotion. The more you express gratitude for what you have the more likely you will have even more to express gratitude for."
— Zig Ziggler

We tend to forget about life's simple blessings such as:
- Salvation and Jesus living in your heart
- Family (spouse, children, parents etc.)
- The roof over your head
- Food
- The gift of life and daily grace
- Clothes
- Transportation

- Talent, jobs, and careers
- Peace of mind
- Health and strength
- The dream you are pursuing
- The list goes on and on

While working toward your life goals, be thankful for all that you do have. So what if you have not achieved all the things tacked to your vision board. Guess what, it could always be worse. Keep working toward your goals, laying a brick every day. Gratitude will make you appreciate where you are and what you have. Hopefully, it will inspire you to keep positively pursuing your dreams. Let's not keep gratifying moments silent. Share them by using the lines on the following page.

The Power of Addition

List the people, things, and experiences you are grateful to have.

I am grateful for...

_____

_____

_____

_____

_____

_____

_____

_____

_____

_____

_____

THANK GOD FOR THEM REPEATEDLY!

> LITTLE DID I REALIZE THAT MY DESIRE TO ADD VALUE TO OTHERS WOULD BE THE THING THAT ADDED VALUE TO ME.
>
> ~ John Maxwell

CHAPTER 5

THE POWER OF SUBTRACTION

"Damn right I love the life I live. I went from negative to positive."

~ The Notorious BIG

Did I mention I love God and trap music? In a world of socially conscious lifestyles, we literally have to un-follow people, break habits, and leave unhealthy situations behind in real life to maintain a positive peace of mind. So many people are caught up in the façade of being hard, claiming to be "SAVAGES," and showcasing heartless actions when they really need to soften up!!

Take time to break away and subtract yourself from distractions, especially negative ones. Much like precious possessions, energy is valuable and needs to be protected. Everything that's negative must go! Detox your mind by subtracting, erasing, disconnecting and unplugging from anything negative. We must rid ourselves of anything toxic before we can move to the next level in life. Don't allow anyone to drive away your peace and push you toward negativity! It doesn't matter if it's a friend, colleague, client, family member, child, or spouse. Jeopardizing your happiness is just not worth it. Sometimes you have to move on without them.

The Power of Subtraction

Negative habits and relationships weigh you down, it's your responsibility to subtract and remove heavy, negative weight.

> *Let us lay aside every weight, and the sin which doth so easily beset us, and let us run with patience the race that is set before us, Looking unto Jesus the author and finisher of our faith...*
>
> ~ Hebrews 12:1

One thing I know for sure, real growth is when we start checking and correcting ourselves for the better. It has been said, *to thy own self be true*. Oftentimes, people are quick to point out the flaws of others, yet fail to make the necessary changes to delete negativity from their own lives.

CHECK YOURSELF.

SOMETIME YOU ARE THE TOXIC PERSON. SOMETIMES YOU ARE THE MEAN NEGATIVE PERSON YOU'RE LOOKING TO PUSH AWAY. SOMETIMES THE PROBLEM IS YOU. AND THAT DOESN'T MAKE YOU LESS WORTHY. KEEP ON GROWING. KEEP ON CHECKING YOURSELF. KEEP ON MOTIVATING YOURSELF. MISTAKES ARE OPPORTUNITIES. LOOK AT THEM, OWN THEM, GROW FROM THEM AND MOVE ON. DO BETTER, BE BETTER. YOU'RE HUMAN. IT'S OKAY.

~ Author Unknown

My advice is to do a self-check. The next time you're ready to judge or criticize someone else, look yourself directly in the face and subtract and release any negativity inside you!!! Rid yourself of any bitterness, bad habits, negative thinking, toxic relationships, etc. Do you have eyes of judgment toward others and not yourself? Can you constantly find faults in others but not yourself? Do you bring down others to make yourself feel better? If so, please read the prayer below.

Prayer for cleansing

Lord, renew in me a clean heart and spirit so that I can be filled with love and kindness like you. Cleanse my soul. Subtract any darkness of negativity from my life. Help me to be beautiful from the inside out, free from the contamination of judg-

ment, and negativity. Humble me to recognize the changes I need to make within myself to live a more positive, passionate, and purposeful life. In Jesus name. ~ Amen

My challenge is for you to take the time to recite the prayer and free yourself from anything and anyone that may be weighing you down, even if it's you. The goal is for you to live a more positive, passionate, and purposeful life. Leave judgment to God and allow people to live their lives. Meanwhile, focus on being a better you.

> *Finally, brothers and sisters, whatever is true, whatever is noble, whatever is right, whatever is pure, whatever is lovely, whatever is admirable—if anything is excellent or praisewor-*

thy—think about such things. Whatever you have learned or received or heard from me or seen in me—put it into practice. And the God of peace will be with you.
~ Philippians 4:8-9

Check your environment and the company you keep. Pay attention to how you feel after being around certain people, places, or atmospheres. It's quite simple to detect when something is breaking you down and pulling the life out of you. You can feel it in your body. You just have to be mature and strong enough to SUBTRACT, let go, and not look back. Whatever is bringing your spirit and energy level down, please do yourself a favor and subtract it.

You don't need worthless, whack, negativity weighing down your life!

I can recall experiencing bad energy at a gathering. I came in warm and friendly as I often do. However, I was greeted with cold stares and cold hearts. It immediately brought my energy down. I'm grateful I was smart enough to subtract myself from that space and gravitated towards warm and welcoming vibes. Energy doesn't lie. I encourage you to pay attention to the energy around you and subtract yourself when necessary.

Take a moment to think about the last negative experience you encountered. Think about the bad vibe that filled the air, the swollen chest, confusion, puffy face, or teary eyes that left the air polluted with tension, anger, disappointment, and hate. I'm sure it's not a great memory, as there's a lot of shade and darkness associated with negativity. Release it! Stop entertaining toxic relationships. The heart symbolizes love not hate. Holding on to any form of hurt, anger, un-forgiveness, negativity, or drama is unhealthy, so please let it go!!

Even when you encounter negativity, I encourage you to be mindful of your responses. Hold on to your peace and realize that every negative battle doesn't require attention.

Stay still and let God fight the battle. I challenge you to PAUSE; hold your tongue the next time someone is rude to you.

Usually, it's the hurt people who hurt others. Practice silence and pray for their brokenness. It's important to understand that we don't have to entertain every fight that we are invited to! Those situations are aimed to test our faith. We cannot be surrounded by negative energy and expect to dwell in positivity.

Prayer for releasing Negativity

Heavenly Father, I rebuke negativity of any form from my life. Help me to abandon and eliminate every negative attack that comes my way. Father-God cancel every curse of negativity ever spoken over my life. Give me the strength to dodge and dismiss any form of negativity. Fill me with peace, love, and positivity. In Jesus' name. ~Amen

Now, think about more positive experiences and how pleasant they were. Recall how peaceful, bright, and light the atmosphere felt. Wouldn't you rather be around sunshine as opposed to the darkness of negativity? Be mindful of what you entertain. I personally want to be around people who eat sunshine and live life glowing with warm hearts of happiness.

Energy and vibes are real, ladies and gentlemen. Therefore, we must learn to acknowledge them. I will be the first to admit that it's hard to let go of negative things, habits, lifestyles, and people that we think feel good or that we have become accustomed to letting live in our lives.

Most times, we know what rots our souls to the core, yet we become complacent, ignore our hearts, and allow the negativity to stay. Live a life exuding so much positivity that negative energy and toxic people dissolve because they no longer know how to approach you with negativity and drama because it's beneath you. Like anything that has life, it can't live if we don't feed it. Negativity can't live where it's not fed. The best decision anyone can ever make is to make thy own self a priority.

Thou shalt get thy own $h%T together and leave any form of negativity behind thee.

~ LaShonda Pierce 1:1

Did you hear that scripture? lol Detox your mind and your contact list! Go ahead and unfriend and unfollow some people in real life. I'll Wait! READY, SET, GO!!!

I challenge you to dig deep and to thy own self-be true. Please! List all the negative habits, distractions, and people that you need to remove from your life in order to live a more *positive, passionate, and purposeful* life.

Below are some unfavorable negative habits to subtract (-) from your life are:

- ➩ Arguing
- ➩ Angriness
- ➩ Alcohol/Drugs
- ➩ Back-biting
- ➩ Belittling
- ➩ Bullying
- ➩ Comparison
- ➩ Competing
- ➩ Complaining
- ➩ Doubting
- ➩ Dissing
- ➩ Drama
- ➩ Deceitfulness
- ➩ Egotistical
- ➩ Envy
- ➩ Finger Pointing
- ➩ Greed
- ➩ Gossiping
- ➩ Harshness
- ➩ Hating
- ➩ Insecurity
- ➩ Judgmental
- ➩ Jealousy
- ➩ Mess
- ➩ Maliciousness
- ➩ Moodiness
- ➩ Manipulation
- ➩ Procrastination
- ➩ Rudeness
- ➩ Sabotaging
- ➩ Self-Doubt
- ➩ Stereotyping
- ➩ Stressing

Prayer of Subtraction

Father-God, thank You for another chance to praise your Holy name. Lord, I thank You for giving me the strength and wisdom to acknowledge what I need to subtract from my life.

Lord, I ask for the discipline and courage to remain focused on pursuing my positive, passionate and purposeful lifestyle. Father-God remove all impulses to entertain negative behaviors, negative energy, negative people, negative outbursts, and negative lifestyles that are not pleasing to You.

Most high God help me to move on without negativity and distractions in my life. Lord, grant me the wisdom to help me identify the areas of my life that need improvement and what specifically needs to be subtracted so that I can live a life that is pleasing to You.

Lord God let me look to You for the cleansing of my own heart and soul. Lord, I don't want to judge others. Instead, I want to better myself and be more like You. Father-God let me release the heavyweights and habits that are hindering me from my positive, passionate and purposeful life. Lord, I know You are love and that positive behavior is a direct reflection of me being more like You. Help me be the child of God You'd have me to be. In Jesus' name I pray…
~ Amen.

POSITIVE · PASSIONATE · PURPOSEFUL

Ask yourself the following questions:

What distractions need to be subtracted from my life that are disturbing my progress, peace, and purpose?

_____

_____

_____

_____

_____

_____

How can I prevent myself from falling into negativity?

_____

_____

_____

_____

The Power of Subtraction

Is there chaos in my life? If so, what are the key factors causing it?

_____

_____

_____

_____

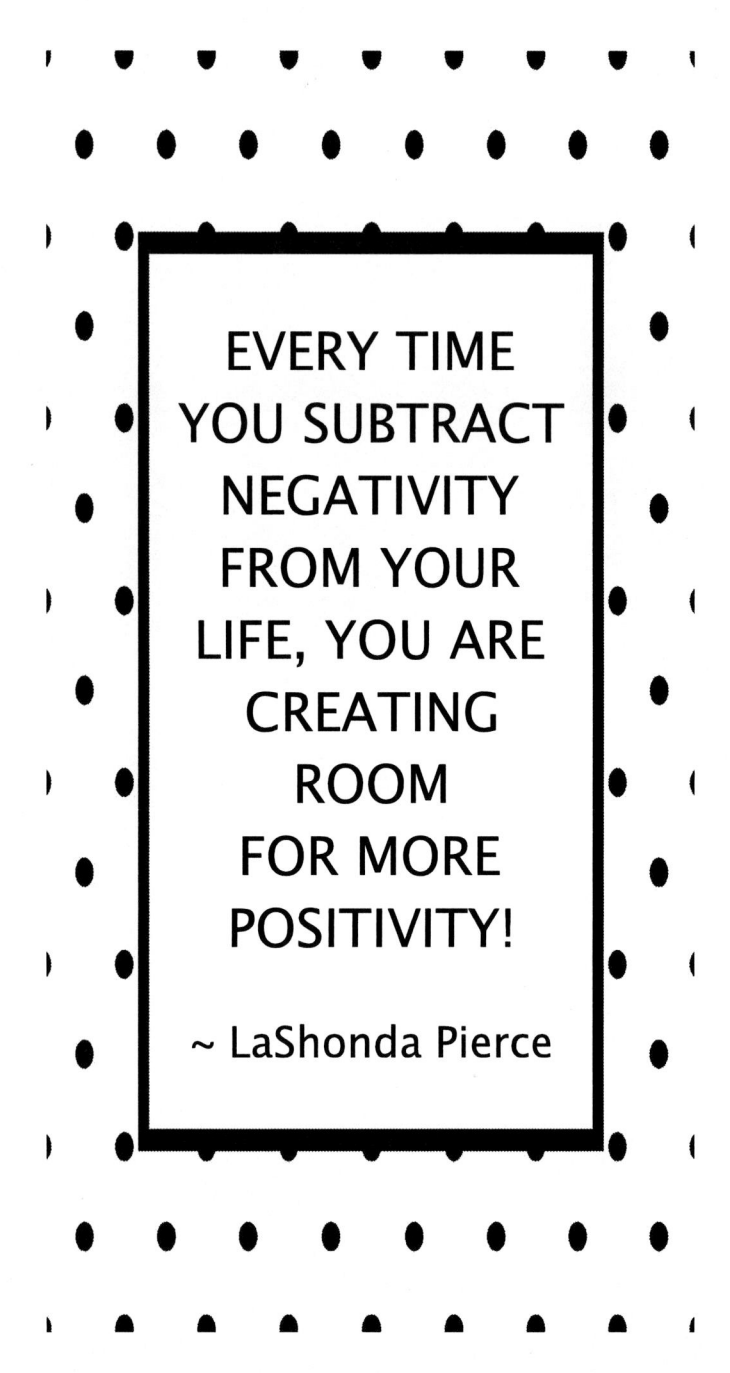

EVERY TIME YOU SUBTRACT NEGATIVITY FROM YOUR LIFE, YOU ARE CREATING ROOM FOR MORE POSITIVITY!

~ LaShonda Pierce

CHAPTER 6

THE POWER OF PERSONAL PEACE

To set the mind on the Spirit is life and Peace.

~ Romans 8:6

Peace is freedom from disturbance — a quiet tranquil place within the mind. It's where you feel calm and undisturbed. It is the result of training your mind to process life as it is rather than as you think it should be. Peace of mind is the cheapest vacation one can take and doesn't require an airplane. I'll take a one-way ticket to personal peace any day! It's extremely important to dwell in personal peace and positivity. Being at peace is the utmost position of power. Your personal peace is your intimate happy place and should always be protected and put first. Personal peace of mind is vital to happiness.

To achieve peace, you must love yourself enough to clear, declutter, and take control of your mind. You must free your mind of chaos, people, places, and habits that aren't good for your personal happiness. Let go of anything that diminishes and breaks your peace. Replace it with the love you deserve.

Self-love is the regard for one's own wellbeing and happiness. You must recognize the importance of peace and self-care and make it non-negotiable. Furthermore, you must recognize the overall happiness it can bring, and add daily rituals that bring joy to your calendar ASAP! This includes holistic behavior for the mind, body and soul.

Taking care of yourself requires unplugging, detaching, and disconnecting in order to connect to your personal peace. You must learn to listen to your body and tap into your own intuition. If you pay attention, your body will provide you with the signals you need. During this time, you should savor in silence and breakaway for a TLC retreat for your own spiritual well-being. This simple task is the key to a healthier and more peaceful you. Consider it a gift to yourself.

Many of us are modern day superheroes, guilty of taking care of everyone else except ourselves. We often fail at making ourselves a priority on our daily to-do lists. For instance, social media has everyone amped about being BOSSES and workaholics believing that the grind needs to be 24-7 and that real bosses don't take days off. Society has idolized the silly thought that it's a bad idea to rest, reset, and recharge. Well, I beg to differ. As an entrepreneur, I use to participate in the no days off movement until my body broke down like an overdriven worn out car. The truth is my body was tired and craving some stillness. We all need to listen to our bodies and get some much-needed rest and rejuvenation. It's ok to relax and recuperate. The grind will be there, but the mind is a terrible thing to waste.

Self-care is the best care. I can recall feeling like a cat chasing its tail — drained, dizzy, and delusional, frankly doing the absolute most. I carried the load of being a mother, entrepreneur, philanthropist, socialite (aka busybody) to where it literally drove me insane. I had to learn to stop. I no longer feel guilty about putting my personal peace first. I am officially over the no days off rule. Yes, work is important in achieving success, but proper rest is vital for personal peace. Don't run your body down trying to prove to clients, coworkers, and social media that you're the hardest worker in the universe. The last time I checked, billions of humans work hard every day. In fact, they have done so for decades before taking pictures of everything became cool. You have nothing to prove to anyone, especially to people on the internet who are not all they "post" themselves to be. Yes, it's great to work, but you must have balance and honor your body with the proper rest and relaxation it deserves.

Release stress and invest in rest!!!

~LaShonda Pierce

Peace is a wealth that money can't buy. You can have all the riches in the world, but if you don't have peace, you're not living your best life! Running rapidly will run you and your body raggedy, both mentally and physically. Proper rest can help remove the frown on your face and bags under your eyes. Learn to be gentle with yourself and identify what your personal peace looks like. Where is that? How does that sound? How does that feel?

For me, it's often solitude and, a quiet time to simply sit still and reflect. So many revelations take place when you pause and embrace moments of solitude. I personally experience more clarity, creativity, moments of gratitude and prioritizing my life. My personal peace usually can be found in a visually appealing room, on a beach listening to waves, or at a park surrounded by beautiful gardens and scenery with greenery. It's important that you too identify what your personal and perfect peace looks like and find time to dwell there.

It's also important to find peace within yourself. Read the Bible, meditate, and pray. Praying is talking to God, meditation is listening to God. We often look to the world and other people to bring us joy and make us happy. The truth is, finding peace is an inside job. Learn to love on yourself, for yourself, by yourself. Being alone makes you strong. Make time to escape the chatter and chaos. I've learned to enjoy my own company, by doing things like:

#1. Spending time with myself, reading and writing.

#2. Taking myself out to dinner.

#3. Enjoying a walk at the park.

#4. Going to see a movie.

#5. Even traveling alone.

When you personally live in peace and accept happiness into your life, you can then share peace with others.

"Remember to take care of yourself. You can't pour from an empty cup."

~ Budah

Here's a thought…

SLOW DOWN!!!

Set some boundaries and stop trying to be everywhere doing everything. Embrace a simple nap, a seat on your sofa and shut down all the mental tabs that are open in your mind. Everything needs proper rest. Cars and machines overheat and need to be turned off, unplugged, and so do you. I'm just here to remind you that the world is already hard on you, so there is no reason that you need to be even harder on your mind, body, and soul.

POSITIVE · PASSIONATE · PURPOSEFUL

Self-care comes in many forms. **If you take the time to treat yourself right, you can then be good for others.** Participating in personal peace and rest can alleviate stress, tension, headaches, crankiness, moodiness, awful attitudes, and an overall poor image.

Below are some suggestions for finding your personal peace:

- Buy a treat
- Dance
- Dream
- Enjoy a spa day
- Enjoy fresh air
- Enjoy music
- Fitness
- Flotation therapy
- Get a massage
- Journal
- Meditate
- Paint
- Rest
- Set boundaries
- Sit Still
- Social media detox

Ask yourself the following questions:

How often do I slow down and connect with personal peace?

_____
_____
_____
_____

When life is stressful, how do I plug into my perfect peace?

_____
_____
_____

In what intimate space do I find personal peace? Describe what that space looks and feels like and then create it!

_____
_____
_____

CHAPTER 7

THE POWER OF PUTTING FAITH OVER FEAR

"For we walk by faith and not by sight."

~ 2 Corinthians 5:7

Faith and fear are total opposites that operate in the same way. They both are fueled by what we think, what we say, and what we act on. It's more valuable and profitable for us to operate in faith. Faith is about doing the best you can and trusting God to do the rest. When you worry, you worship the problem and dishonor God. The worry syndrome typically ends when your faith in God kicks in. Fear is when you forget that God is in charge!! You can't worry and trust God at the same time. You've just got to FAITH it until you make it!

Fear is not from God and we shouldn't live our lives being afraid. Often times worry and stress can create problems that were never there to begin with. Stress is a negative feature and subtracts from your life and can cause you to:

Lose Hope
Lose Hair
Lose Weight
Lose Ambition

The Power of Faith

Which can ULTIMATELY make you lose money because you can't focus on being your best self. Extreme stress and depression can intensify the risk of early death. Stop allowing worry to take over your thoughts and valuable time. The anxiety just isn't worth it.

Be a Warrior, not a Worrier!

~ Author Unknown

We must put our faith in God and trust that the answers to our prayers are on the way.

For example, trusting God is similar to being an Amazon Prime customer. Members receive benefits which include FREE fast shipping; member's trust that their packages are on the way, and are confident of the delivery.

I'm here to remind you that God is far more reliable than Amazon prime. He may not come when you want Him but he's always right on time. When I think back over my life, I'm reminded of the countless times I've had to simply do what I can, then get out of the way, let go, and let God.

Every time my back has been against the wall He's showed up and showed out. Blessing and keeping me, by putting me on the heart of someone at the right time to receive a super natural blessing perfectly packaged and delivered from Him to me. Aligning me and my business with mind blowing opportunities… God never leaves or forsakes us; he's always right on time.

With God on our side opportunities and access will be granted, and supernatural ways are made.

Stop allowing worry to take over your thoughts and valuable time, let go and let God.

Be Positive, Stay Passionate and Live Purposefully

I believe the true power in putting faith over fear is the ability to program the mind to see the best in everything. A positive mindset is a choice and a perspective. It may sound cliché, but we should always believe that something wonderful is going to happen. Faith is knowing and trusting that God has millions of unimaginable ways to turn your situation around outside of your reach.

Just because you don't see a way right now doesn't mean God doesn't have a way. Look for the pot of gold on the other side of the rainbow. We must put our faith in

God and trust that the answer to your prayer is on the way.

I want to be very clear that great things happen in life because of the obvious — hard work and positive attitudes. The Bible tells us in James 2:20 that faith without work is dead. We can't pray and not do the work.

The positive attitude inspires hard work. Many of us lose our faith due to not trusting God's timing. We want things to happen overnight. Unfortunately, it's just not going to happen that way. Although it may be a slow process, we must not let time make us quit and distrust what God promised would happen. God wouldn't allow us to have a vision if it wouldn't come to pass; we have to continue to work and trust.

We must learn to hold the vision, strategize a plan, trust the process, and embrace the journey. Things may not go at the speed we often desire, but quitting certainly won't speed up the process.

> ***I want to see what happens,***
> ***if I don't give up.***
>
> ~Author Unknown

Think back to the childhood story of *The Little Engine That Could*. "I think I can. I think I can."

Pep talks are positive affirmations spoken over our lives. Moreover, they are reminders to be and pursue greatness.

What are you telling yourself during your trying times? (Are you the little engine that could? I think I can. I think I can.)

Thinking and living positively is PARAMOUNT to faith. It's trusting and believing that everything will work out for the best. Faith is having complete trust or confidence in something. It's a strong belief in God.

I remember when it was hard for me to remain positive. How was I, the positivity cheerleader, not practicing what I preached? **Where were my positive pants and megaphone?** I was a walking pity party, feeling defeated, and not very optimistic. I was faced with several adversities at once and things just weren't going my way. My finances were depleted, my love story had ended, I questioned my career, and quite frankly didn't see much value in myself.

As a result, I was afraid, distracted, and burdened by stress. I would walk around feeling gloomy and low in spirits. That difficult time darkened my life, my mind, my spirit, and my motivation for living my best life.

When things aren't going great or at the speed you'd hope for, it can lead to negative thinking which can lead to depression and self-sabotaging. There is nothing positive associated with depression. I'm proud to say through prayer and positive thinking I was able to shake that negative load I was carrying and shine the positive light back into in my life. By praying and thinking positive, I reinvented my life. I did inventory over my life and all of the positive contributions I add to the universe.

I reminded myself of all of the positive attributes within me and told myself, ok, I may not be financially free; however, I'm filthy rich in spirit. I'm compassionate, creative, and my gifts and talents add value to the lives of those I serve. I'm a great encourager and cheerleader of others. Yes, I went through the disappointment of a breakup but so does everyone one else. I learned to practice non-attachment and accepting what comes and allowing it to leave when it's time.

My faith was really tested during this time. I was raised in the Baptist church, so I know all about the power of prayer and faith, but somehow, I'd fallen short of trusting God's promises. Being faith-filled is a positive characteristic. I reprogrammed my mind into trusting that I would get through tough times. I took advantage of my not so great situations and grew into a better person from them.

How we handle adversities says a lot about how much faith we have. Do we give up or keep pushing ourselves? Real winners are in it to win it. Winners push themselves to their best potential. We can't let a negative setback keep us down. Beyoncé's freedom verse says it best: "Ima keep running 'cause a winner don't quit on themselves." Yes, we will fall into unpleasant times, but we must never quit!!

I'm reminded of a demonstration with an egg and a ball. When the egg hits the floor it cracks, shatters, and becomes a complete mess, yet when a ball hits the floor it bounces right back. In life, yes we will fall, but I want to encourage you to bounce back up. **#dontcrackunderpressure**

Remember, planes are always grounded before takeoff, be okay with being at the bottom from time to time.
Your lift off is on God's schedule.

~LaShonda Pierce

I often encourage friends to be mad as opposed to sad when going through tough times. When you're sad you are fragile, weak, and basically in a fetal position. It's easy for depression to arise or self-doubt, lack of ambition, etc. When we're sad, we look in the mirror with low confidence.

Yet when we're mad, fighting mad, (the kind of mad where your fists are clenched and the rocky soundtrack plays in your head) you can see the champion within yourself and it brings out the best in you; it helps you turn pain into power and becomes the fuel to your fire. Pain and problems motivate and brings out the fighter and champion within me. Allow them to do the same for you.

We have to encourage ourselves, during those not so good times, give ourselves pep talks. Be reminded of exactly who you are and why you exist and allow the true champion within you to arouse. Be the warrior you truly are.

> *A just man falls seven times and rises up again*
>
> ~ Proverbs 24:16

"GOD HEARD YOUR PRAYERS. GOD CAN FEEL YOUR PAIN. HE KNOWS THAT YOU ARE OVERWHELMED, EXHAUSTED, AND WORRIED ABOUT HOW EVERYTHING IS GOING TO WORK OUT. GOD IS SAYING TO YOU TODAY, "TRUST ME" I WILL GET YOU THROUGH THIS SEASON. I WILL FIX WHAT IS BROKE. REST IN ME."

~ Author unknown

The Power of Faith

As Christians, we have been commanded to live by faith and not to fear, worry, or stress. Living by faith is remaining calm through adversity, sorrow, despair, or any negative situation that arises. It's trusting God through EVERYTHING — every circumstance, every trial, every setback, every dilemma, and everything that is meant to knock you down.

Your faith and positive mindset allow you to keep going and keep believing that brighter days are coming. Fear-free people live a more relaxed life by breaking the habit of worrying knowing that God is in control. One touch of God's favor can change your entire situation. Stay faithful and trust His timing in your life.

You must increase your faith daily. Rebuild your life, refocus, and redirect your energy. Recharge your faith and move forward by not getting stuck on worry. I'm reminded of the saying, "I don't look like what I've been through" (or what I'm going through for that matter). There's beauty in keeping calm during a storm and realizing how to see favor while in the furnace.

> *For therein is the righteousness of God revealed from faith to faith: as it is written, the just shall live by faith.*
>
> ~ Romans 1:17

Have you ever looked back over your life and seen the message in the mess? I can recall losing a job. As a result, that forced me to have faith and really pursue my dream of entrepreneurship. I can also recall a friend being heartbroken after a divorce only to realize God had her true dream man on the other side of her pain. Perhaps you were denied a job, but a few months later God blessed you with something better than you imagined. Faith is about trusting God and watching Him wow and amaze you. God laughs at the little dreams and plans we have for ourselves because He wants to bless us with so much more. We just have to have faith the size of the mustard seed and believe. Faith is really believing in yourself and the works of God.

The moment we awake, we must program our mind and decide that it will be a great day! Make a habit of speaking positive affirmations over your life and having FAITH that they will indeed come true.

CHAPTER 8

THE POWER OF STAYING POSITIVE (IN SPITE OF...)

Life is filled with ups and downs, and will throw all kinds of curve balls our way ; making it easy to fall into the left field of negative thoughts during difficult times. There are good and bad chapters in our life stories. It's important we embrace the beauty of discomfort and receive the vital message in the mess.

Every tough experience is mastering you at becoming a better you. Experiences, whether good or bad, provide wisdom and can be a testimony to help someone else facing similar situations. Life can be picture perfect one day and a whirlwind of changes the next. Please don't let negative experiences dictate and determine your outlook on life. Even car batteries need positive and negative terminals to operate properly. Much like film, we can develop from negative situations. I wish that we lived a life without adversities, mistakes, and pain. However, that's only wishful thinking. We all fall short of God's glory. We get lost, fail at something, and go through trial and error. Often, God will disrupt our lives to get our undivided attention and sometimes that means trouble in paradise. Through every trial, there is a valuable lesson.

"Let me tell you something you already know. The world isn't all sunshine and

rainbows. It's a very mean and nasty place, and I don't care how tough you are. It will beat you to your knees and keep you there permanently if you let it. You, me, or nobody is going to hit as hard as life."

~ Rocky Balboa

Staying positive in a negative world is like wearing proper armor in a war or a warm coat in the winter. It's a necessary layer of protection. I truly believe that facing adversity is one of life's best hands-on lessons. Negative experiences help shape and define our character and help us to build strength. We can't fold under pressure. The pressures of life are inevitable, but it's how we handle difficult situations that test our faith and determine our maturity. We've got to boss up and tune in to

POSITIVE · PASSIONATE · PURPOSEFUL

our inner strength during difficult times. Learn to *remain positive, stay passionate, and live purposefully...*

> *In spite of altercations*
> *In spite of heartbreaking losses*
> *In spite of health issues*
> *In spite of financial challenges*
> *In spite of failed relationships*
> *In spite of difficulties*
> *In spite of loneliness*
> *In spite of whatever*

You can still overcome and win!!

Don't put too much energy into something that will ultimately lower your spiritual vibration. Take a deep breath, face the issue, and welcome the future. Be positive and believe in yourself and the power of God.

When faced with adversity, you'll be amazed at the strength and resilience living on the inside of you. Strength is ignited if you remain positive, stay passionate, and continue to live purposely.

I can recall my first up close and personal experience with major health crises. During this time, I personally saw three beautiful women living everyday lives suddenly faced with the unannounced war of cancer and health challenges. I witnessed my friends battle both breast and oral cancer and another nearly losing her eyesight. Within reason, this would have shambled a lot of people whether male or female. **THROUGH IT ALL,** I observed them display so much grace, strength, and beauty all while on the battlefield of life, remaining positive in spite of.

So many people deal with the uncertainties of life. Therefore, it's important to pour positive energy into the spirits of those we encounter. The statistics on health, divorce, death, depression, suicide, etc., are real. Everyone is going through something, yet the world keeps spinning like a never-ending merry-go-round. Since we can't stop the ride and get off, we've got to learn to manage the circles and cycles of life by staying positive.

We can all make a difference in someone's life by simply being kind and positive shining light in darkness. Sending words of encouragement, being kind, sharing a friendly smile to a stranger and lending an ear to a friend are all ways to shine your light. These simple gestures can make a difference in someone's life. It's important to stay positive in:

- A crisis
- Your marriage
- Your workplace
- Relationships
- Organizations
- Church
- Etc.

Haven't heard from someone? Check on them. Even your strongest friends, who seem to have it all together, face challenges. A smile on a pretty picture can mask a lot of pain and brokenness. Being gentle and positive with others can have an enormous impact in someone's life. The world we live in can be dark and cruel.

High functioning depression is a real thing.

Check on your... hilarious ass, smiling ass, positive ass, inspirational ass, boss ass friends.

~Author Unknown

We must constantly remind others that they're magical. You just may be saving someone's soul. Remember to gas people up, encourage them, and magnify their spirit.

Whenever someone seeks advice from me while facing a challenge, my response is to keep calm, trust God, and remain positive. We can't revert to a toddler and have temper tantrums when things don't go our way. We have to take the high road, grow up, and go with the flow. Grow and evolve from what you go through.

If you have yet to experience anything, look at the resilience of survivors all around you and pray for that same strength. Realize that quitting is not an option. You're a survivor with overcoming power on the inside of you. Use that God-given power to rise above every situation and circumstance.

Allow the struggle to be fuel to the fire. We are all faced with the adversities of life in one way or another. We must allow adversity to ignite the champion within us. We've got to keep moving. Yes, I know it hurts. But it will change you for the better.

I am often faced with challenge after challenge. Through experience, I'm reminding you it's better to be mad and not sad about situations. Anger often causes us to fight for our rights. It reminds us of our value and the amazing person that we are. We're not fighting in a negative way. Instead, we are internally fighting (you vs. you) to be our best while proving the enemy wrong.

You'd be surprised at how much motivation a broken heart can give you. I challenge you to use those hurtful, unpleasant situations to cause you to lift off like a rocket and soar to higher heights. Let that breakup make you better, not bitter. Allow your lack of finances today make you a better steward tomorrow. Whatever you're facing — health risks, unemployment, foreclosure, bankruptcy, divorce or the death of a loved one, allow it to bring you to a place of peace and hope for the future.

In life, you will have humble beginnings and unexpected ends. The key is to never forget that you can start over, or late and finish strong. You can try, fail, and still succeed, just don't quit!

Don't allow what you are going through to block where you are going to. God is preparing you for something great! Sometimes bills add up, you lose a job, a relationship ends, you lose a friendship, you encounter an unexpected loss — life isn't always great but always remember that the pain that you have been feeling can't compare to the joy that's coming.

There are two types of pains — pain that hurts you and pain that changes you.

Speak positive affirmations over your life; promote and push yourself until it pays off. Use every opportunity to become better. Refrain from negativity because it's subtracting from your life, not adding.

POSITIVE · PASSIONATE · PURPOSEFUL

10 Affirmations to Start the Day

1. I will greet the day with ease.
2. I am in charge of my thoughts.
3. I wake up with a peaceful mind and grateful heart.
4. I will not worry about things out of my control.
5. The sunrise fills me with love, light, and strength.
6. I will find joy in the simple pleasures of life.
7. Everything I need will come to me at the right time.
8. I will put faith over fear.
9. I will live my life with love, kindness and gratitude.
10. Today is filled with amazing possibilities.

PRAYER TO STAY POSITIVE IN SPITE OF

Father-God, I bring my burdens to You as you know my heavy heart and situation. I can't make it in this negative world without Your protective armor around me. Comfort my heart and give me the strength to carry on. Help me to be positive in spite of, stay passionate, and live purposefully.

In Jesus' name, Amen

Ask yourself the following questions:

What are the benefits of positive affirmations?

_____

_____

What lessons can be learned from the challenges of life?

_____

_____

How can I grow from a negative experience?

_____

_____

How does a negative experience strengthen me?

_____

_____

CHAPTER 9

THE POWER OF POSITIVE FRIENDS

"Show me your friends and I'll show you your future.'

~ Chaplain Ronnie Melancon

'm going to start this chapter off by saying you and God are your two closest friends; everyone else is a bonus. Having friends and allowing people into your life is great, but ultimately you need to cherish and depend on yourself and the unwavering hand of God.

There will be times when you will be an army of one, fighting silent battles that aren't posted on social media and dealing with private moments that aren't so pretty. Late at night in the midnight hour when it's just you, your fears, heartache, and tears...There will be days when your back is against the wall and Jesus is the only one you can call.

Jesus will show up (often not in the timing or way that you expect) it can very well be an angel in the form of an encouraging word through another, a good deed, sermon, etc. He's a present God in the time of trouble. Wherever there is difficulty — in the courtroom, classroom, hospital, work place, etc. Whenever I feel as though I'm an army of one, I have a beautiful reminder that in Christ I can find comfort and I know that with Him, I am not alone. He will always guide me and ultimately be the very best friend that I could ever have.

Unlike family, your friends are handpicked. The privileges of having friends are amazing. You connect due to similarities, interests, and lifestyles. There's an old saying: birds of a feather flock together.

We create amazing memories and have so much fun with our friends. However, there comes a time when you have to evaluate your life and the people in it. Sometimes, you have to take an inventory of your friendships and separate the people who add value to your life from those who don't. Do the math. Subtract where necessary, then add and attach yourself to greatness.

This can be difficult, but it needs to happen a few times during your life. We never stop growing and evolving. Time will tell who should stay and go. Interests change, people change, priorities change, and lifestyles change. We must be receptive to change.

Your future is often influenced or affected by those closest to you. Often, we are guilty by association. Whether good or bad, things come to you based on who you're connected to. Therefore, it's vital to check the connections of the company you keep.

Characteristics, habits, and mindsets can easily rub off by association. We must surround ourselves with three types of people:

The Positive, The Passionate, and The Purposeful. Your inner circle, your crew, your clique, or your squad (whichever context best resonates with you) should be influential to your life. These individuals should love, trust, and challenge you for the better.

Your friends should have a variety of skills, personalities, and talents. Your interactions should be purposeful, and not just for indulging in pleasure and socializing. Your conversations should be about goals and growth, and not gossip and parties.

I think that it is important to know, to have a friend is to be a friend. What kind of friend are you? Are you supportive, kind, encouraging, and loyal? Mr. Jimmy Rex said it best: "Be the type of friend you want to be friends with." I try to live by this motto.

KEEP POSITIVE PEOPLE AROUND YOU OR BE ALONE…

~LaShonda Pierce

I recently read, friends that "Aye" when you dance are so important. This comment made me smile as it resonated with me. Yes, we do need friends that say "Aye" and "Yay"when we dance, but we also need them to keep that same energy while we are chasing our dreams, pursuing our purpose, sealing deals, and working hard.

We are equivalent to the five people we spend the most time with. You should be connected to people that genuinely want to see you win in life and vice versa — people who will pull out their megaphones and pompoms and cheer for you like they do for celebrities and people they don't know.

Pour into your friends so that they can grow and develop. You can't call yourself a friend and be silent when your friends have great news, or laugh and smirk when they have bad news. Neither can you be around chickens expecting to soar like an eagle.

If you're around people who are comfortable with mediocrity, offended by your ambition or those who that drain the life, love, and happiness out of you, then you can't possibly be in position to live your best life. If your friendships don't challenge you to change for the better, that's likely not a positive, passionate, and purposeful friendship.

Your real friends will travel with you during the ups and downs of life. Cherish and cheer for people, and give people their flowers while they are alive and can smell them. Especially your friends. It's sad that life doesn't bring people together like

The Power of Positive Friends

death does. It's too late to celebrate the life of a loved one when they're dead and gone. There is no room for unsupportive relationships. Much like there are love languages in marriages, they are also valid in friendships. I encourage you to communicate with your friends when you feel a shift or a disconnect. Real friendships are worth fighting for. We only have one life. Keep it simple.

- ➢ If you're missing somebody, call.
- ➢ If you want to meet up, invite.
- ➢ If you want to be understood, cxplain.
- ➢ If you have questions, ask.
- ➢ If you don't like something, speak up.

- If you like something, share it.
- If you want something, ask for it.
- If you love someone, tell them.

I can recall feeling let down by people I loved and it was hard to remain positive about the friendship. I was expecting them to love and support me the way I loved and supported them. Support isn't always financial, sometimes it's the little things. I needed genuine concern, calls, and words of encouragement. Instead, I felt left out, excluded, and let down. My expectations had me on a roller coaster. I was all up in my feelings, then down in the dumps. It's been said that sometimes we expect so much from others because we'd be willing to do so much for them.

> *"Thats why I'm so Harsh...because I'm so sensitive "*
> —Tupac Shakur

I have since learned to manage my expectations. Once I realized what I was feeling had nothing to do with them, but everything to do with me, my vibrations changed. Expectations are powerful; you must remove expectations from people and by doing so you'll remove their power to hurt you.

Truth is, we all love differently based on our upbringing and the environment we were raised in. Some people are emotional, affectionate, and considerate, and some are not. This doesn't mean that they don't care about you. It just means you have to be able to effectively communicate your expectations and personal love languages of how you wish to be loved.

We must stop expecting so much from people we haven't been upfront with. Have the courage to have those conversations. Now, if you have communicated your needs and they've been ignored, it's okay to remove yourself from that situation. You deserve better. But ultimately you should manage and communicate your expectations.

Dear God,

If I hurt others, give me the strength to apologize. If people hurt me give me the strength to forgive. Amen

I'm grateful to have a great group of friends. They are with me for great laughs, yet they challenge me for the better. We talk about everything from politics, to dreams, to careers, life, etc. I can recall jokingly calling a couple of my friends my "parole officers". I was enjoying my "Sunday Fun day" a little too much, and they quickly got me all the way together. I wasn't dancing on the table or swinging from the chandeliers but let's just say I was getting there.

I may fuss, but I thank God for good friends like that. Surround yourselves with people who believe in and want the best for you. You need friends who love you enough to tell you what you don't necessarily want to hear. Instead, they tell you what's in your best interest. I can't express how important it is to be around people that genuinely care for you, people who make you feel special and appreciated. True friendships are mutual and immeasurable. Surround yourself with people who love, value, and respect your point of view, and the gift of your friendship.

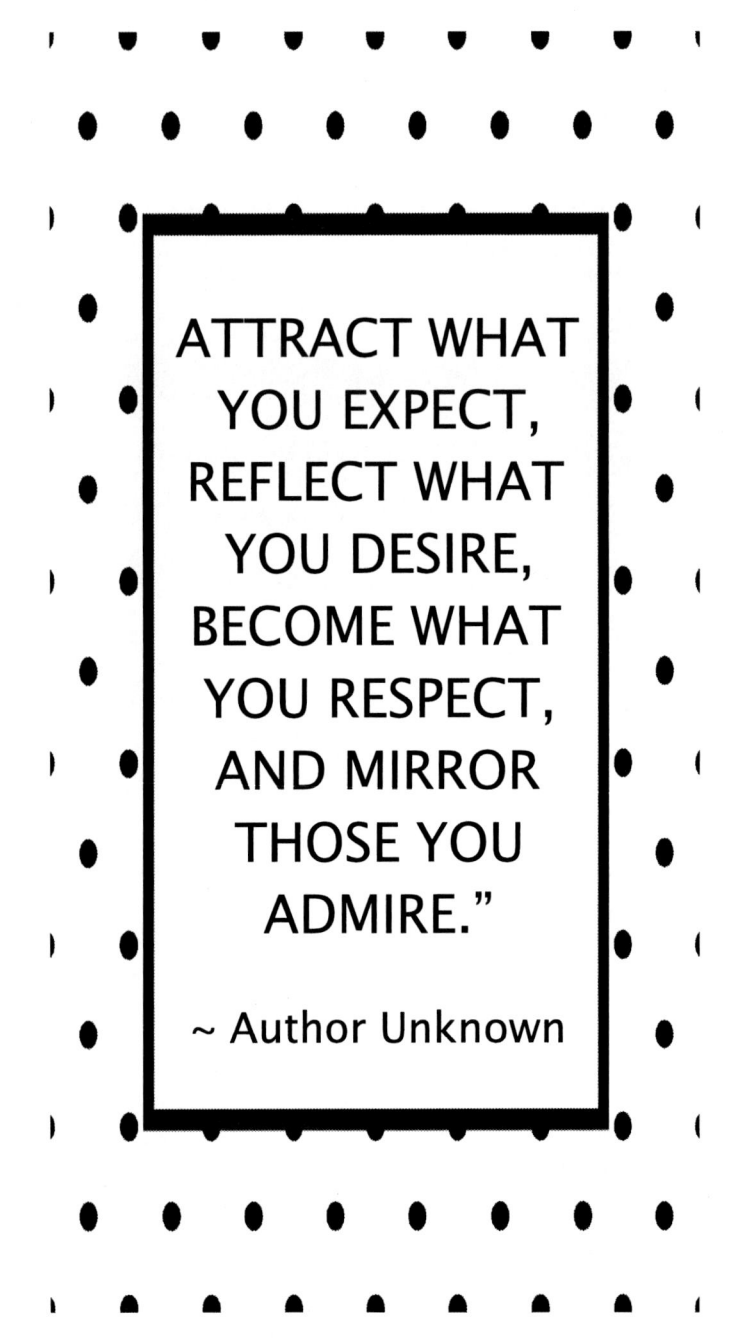

ATTRACT WHAT YOU EXPECT, REFLECT WHAT YOU DESIRE, BECOME WHAT YOU RESPECT, AND MIRROR THOSE YOU ADMIRE."

~ Author Unknown

Friends who defend you in your absence, check on you when your quiet, and communicate mutually. Friends who will be honest with you, even when it's hard. Friends who encourage you to ignite your passions, celebrate your talents and push you toward your dreams. Friends who are selfless and give without expecting anything in return.

Be sure to surround yourself with people who choose you. Those are your people, love those who love you. Give yourself permission to separate yourself from those who don't. We all deserve beautiful friendships that are not hurtful, or questionable... because true friendships are mutual and immeasurable .

To live your best life, I suggest removing yourself from people and situations that stunt your growth, harm your heart, and hinder your happiness. Pay attention to who claps when you make a home run and who kneels to help you when you've fallen.

Positive relationships should flow like a river. Life is too short to waste with people who don't appreciate you. It's okay to keep them in your heart but out of your life. Rid yourselves of relationships that keep you from flourishing.

Be grateful for the people in your life that love growing, evolving, excelling, and encourage you to do the same. Consider those individuals your circle of success.

I know that there are some people who will say that they don't want or have any friends. If you don't have a group of friends who motivate you toward success or you haven't found a mentor that's perfect for your life.

The Power of Positive Friends

If lack of funds is prohibiting you from hiring an amazing life coach, try looking on the internet — it's a powerful resource.

There are friends at your fingertips via Google, podcasts, blogs, vlogs and various social media platforms. I follow all sorts of people from all over the world, industry greats, business moguls, average Joes, local celebrities, and more. I follow positive, productive people that can impact my life in some way or another. I encourage you to do the same.

It's necessary to stretch yourself, step outside your ordinary circle, add diversity, and meet some new people with successful track records and accomplishments.

What does that mean? SURROUND YOURSELF WITH THE GREATS! Network with the right people. There are pictures and biographies of celebrities and people I admire in frames around my home as if I know them.

I know it may sound silly to some, but I'm surrounding myself with the greats. I familiarize myself with their successful habits. I research and learn how they've gained success. I know their stories and how they reached the level of success I'm striving to attain. This is a great way to gain knowledge and better yourself.

When you're positive, happy, and striving for your best, you and those around you benefit. It's like a domino effect. The effect we have on each other is valuable and has an enormous impact on our lives. Be mindful that positivity has the potential to spread in the same way that negativity does. Relationships should either evolve or dissolve. Expect more, increase the value of your life, and surround yourself with GOOD ENERGY and Good People that love you no matter where you are in life!!

> *Walk with the wise and become wise, for a companion of fools suffers harm.*
>
> ~ Proverbs 13:20

Ask yourself the following questions:

Who are your closest friends?

_____
_____
_____
_____

(Celebrate them every chance you get!)

Who do you admire and why?

_____
_____
_____
_____

Who's your most valued friend and why?

_____
_____
_____
_____

The Power of Positive Friends

Who holds you accountable and stretches you to your best potential??

_____
_____
_____
_____

Who's the most successful person you know personally?

_____
_____
_____
_____

What do you learn from that person?

_____
_____
_____
_____

BE POSITIVE · STAY PASSIONATE · LIVE PURPOSEFULLY

#Thank God for good friends!

CHAPTER 10

THE POWER OF IGNITING YOUR PASSION

"Do not choose the lesser life. Do you hear me? Do you hear me? Choose the life that is yours, the life that is seducing your lungs, that is dripping down your chin."

~ Nayyirah Waheed

When I think of passion, I think of the heart throbbing, exhilarating feeling I get when I'm in my zone doing what I love. I'm adrenalized during the moments of promoting positivity, designing a space, creating custom furniture, or clothing! Being in your personal element is a feeling full of acceleration and hunger that sets your soul on fire! I encourage you to acknowledge your zone of genius, ignite it and share it with the world.

Passion isn't questionable; it's evident and clear. There is something special when you do what you were born to do. No one will be able to recognize your calling like you. Much like Lebron James on the basketball court, Beyoncé and Bruno Mars on a stage, or P Diddy in the studio, you pour your heart and soul into what you love. You exude what you love without having to say much because it's unmistakably evident in what you do.

Your purpose provokes your passion.

> *"Stop chasing the money
> and start chasing the passion."*
>
> ~ Tony Hsieh

When you're truly passionate about something, it takes primacy over anything else and captivates your attention. If you're truly passionate about it, (whatever "it" is) you will be doing a lot of it! When you truly love something, you will find and make time for it.

For instance, when I'm creating a space, promoting positivity, empowering the community, my heart is in it. My passion allows me to connect on a deeper level. Your passion strengthens you to work early mornings and late nights, often for free because you love it so much. None of those things matter when you're doing what you love.

POSITIVE · PASSIONATE · PURPOSEFUL

Outside of positivity, I'm passionate about fashion and interior design. My mission is to ensure that people look and live beautifully. That's my happy place! When I was a kid, I loved styling paper dolls. They were my greatest joy. I can remember using a large J.C. Penney catalog and selecting my favorite outfits to cut out makeshift paper dolls when my store-bought books were depleted.

To this day, my soul still gets happy from a simple $5 magazine full of great fashions and furnishings. ***It's no accident the excitement you feel about something you truly love. Pay attention to what sets your soul on fire.***

I moved in with my grandmother Geneva at age thirteen. She is a talented seamstress and made most of my clothing.

Dresses, pants, socks you name it, Geneva could sew it. As a teenager, I couldn't appreciate or understand that living with my grandmother and watching her sew my wardrobe was preparing me for a future in design. What I considered a fashion disgrace, prepared me for a love and career in fashion and textiles. GO FIGURE!

I can remember dreading weekly trips to fabric and vintage shops, designing clothing with my grandmother and constantly redecorating my room. These experiences helped shape and tailor LaPierce Designs. Now, I live every day in my element, ensuring that people look and live beautifully!

I can now laugh at how I made shopping miracles with a limited income. In fact, it taught me how to be creative and stretch a dollar — making a little go a long way.

I can recall winning best dressed in high school with a mere $64 government check, bargain and vintage shopping.

Fast forward to now being a designer and clients asking me if I can create a design on a dime. Well heck yeah, of course, I can! I'm a certified, qualified, and experienced deal finder!! Bargain shopping is my passion!

There will be a variety of things you will be passionate about in your lifetime, but the key is to allow your passion to drive you to your destiny and God-given purpose! Ask God to reveal the thirst in your life. Be thirsty for the next level that God has for you.

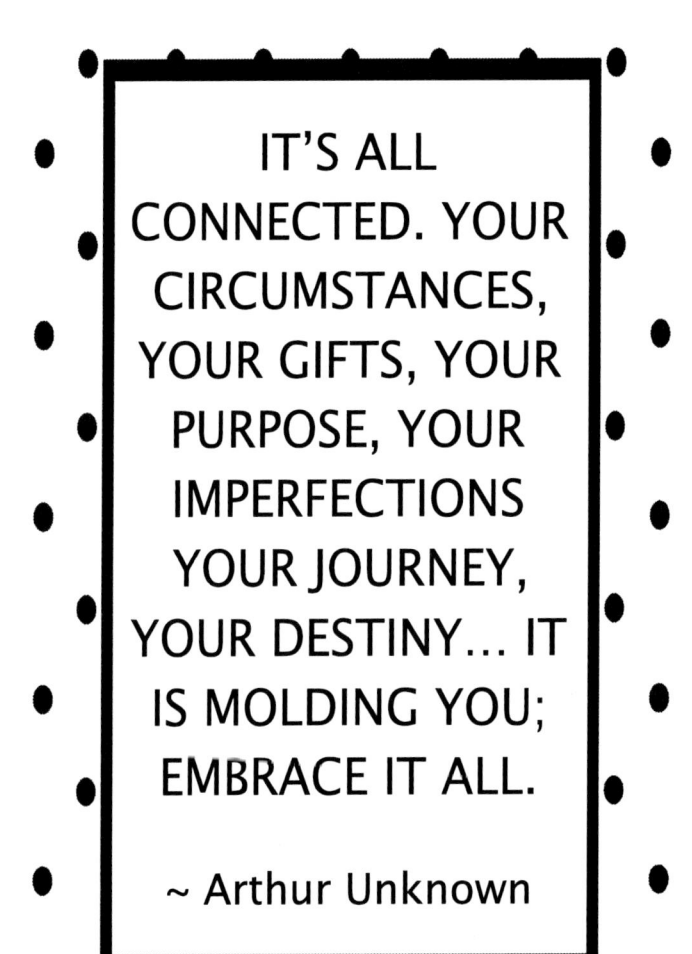

IT'S ALL CONNECTED. YOUR CIRCUMSTANCES, YOUR GIFTS, YOUR PURPOSE, YOUR IMPERFECTIONS YOUR JOURNEY, YOUR DESTINY... IT IS MOLDING YOU; EMBRACE IT ALL.

~ Arthur Unknown

START LIVING YOUR MOST PASSIONATE LIFE NOW!

To identify your passion, you must recognize what's thriving in your heart and what you are in love with. No matter what your age, you'll never have it if you don't pursue it. Don't allow yourself to live with unfulfilled potential that's ready to be ignited. Dig deep into yourself and understand who you are, what you want, and what ignites your heart.

Follow your calling. Do the things that excite your soul. Is it the arts or something creative? Is it in ministry, beauty, or perhaps health and wellness? There is a plethora of passions to consider. Just allow your soul and spirit to be the guiding force in your life.

Determine and acknowledge your calling, hone in on your strengths, and make your passion your reality. Sharing your passion with the world can also bring financial prosperity and wealth to your life. There are numerous people who have benefited financially from doing things that they love and are passionate about.

It's not out of the ordinary to identify your true passion later in life. I see it all the time. I know a successful electrical engineer whose true passion is art, as well as a hairstylist who craves a life of interior design. Many people have chosen lucrative careers over their true passion. It's actually smart to start that way. Just know it's never too late to follow and pursue your dreams. Pay attention to what you do well and what makes your soul happy and **JUST**

DO IT! ALLOW YOUR PASSION TO SET YOU APART!

May your gifts and talents be your game changer.

~LaShonda Pierce

PRAYER FOR DISCOVERING YOUR PASSION

Heavenly Father, thank you for my personal gifts, abilities, and talents. Lord, thank You for making me unique and special. Father-God, I pray for the wisdom to discover and develop my passion and live a life designed specifically for me. Help me to pursue my dreams, honor my passion, and utilize the gifts you've so richly blessed me with to share with the world the best way I can.

~In Jesus' name, Amen

> WHEN I STAND BEFORE GOD AT THE END OF MY LIFE, I WOULD HOPE THAT I WOULD NOT HAVE A SINGLE BIT OF TALENT LEFT AND COULD SAY, I USED EVERYTHING YOU GAVE ME.
>
> ~ Erma Bombech

Ask yourself the following questions:

What childhood experiences have shaped you to become who you are today?

_____

_____

_____

_____

What could you spend the rest of your life doing?

_____

_____

_____

_____

What are your strengths?

_____

_____

_____

_____

What is your unique gift or talent?

_____
_____
_____
_____

What do you feel you were born to do?

_____
_____
_____
_____

What fears or barriers are stopping you from pursuing your passion?

_____
_____
_____
_____
_____

POSITIVE · PASSIONATE · PURPOSEFUL

How can you impact the world by sharing your passion?

_____
_____
_____
_____
_____
_____

What actions are you going to take to begin living out your passion?

_____
_____
_____
_____
_____
_____

Are you going to build or bull $hit? The choice is yours. #Let's go!

CHAPTER 11

THE POWER OF LIVING PURPOSEFULLY

"Your talent is God's gift to you. What you do with it is your gift back to God."

~ Leo Buscaglia

Living a purposeful life is the best gift anyone can personally give themselves. A purposeful individual doesn't hold back; they live an extraordinary life of IMPACT and INFLUENCE. They walk it like they talk it by putting action behind their dreams. Purposeful people aren't stagnant. They don't stop! They get it. Get it! Even when the going gets tough, they keep going.

> *Each of you should use whatever gift you have received to serve others, as faithful stewards of God's grace in its various forms.*
>
> ~ 1 Peter 4:10

Think of your purpose as a divine life assignment from God. God is a designer and has tailored each of us unique and extraordinary, with a specific purpose and calling for our lives. We all have special gifts and talents inside of us that we should honor and share with the world. What assignment has God placed in your life? Close your eyes and meditate on that for a moment.

Think back to the previous chapter where we identified your passions, gifts, and talents, then lace up your mind and shoes and begin walking in your purpose!! That my friend is your divine assignment. The world is depending on you, so don't hold back your magic, live purposefully, do what God has called you to do!

Our purpose is what we were specifically designed to do in life. Purposeful individuals are authentic, fearless, focused, forward-moving people who set the standard of excellence for their lives. God created each of us unique and special. The one thing nobody has the power to be is you. Celebrate who you are.

The beauty in personal purpose is that we each have our own vision, ethics, voice, mind, and story that only we can live out. We all are pregnant with purpose on the inside of us. We don't need a surrogate to bring our purpose to life. We only need to **PUSH** our dreams out into the universe. Regardless of similarities, no one can walk in your purpose like you.

I'm honored to walk in my personal purpose every day. I hope that in some way my life encourages others to pursue their personal purpose as well. I know that I was created to *ensure that people look and live beautifully*.

For instance, Interior Design is much more than fluffing pillows and matching colors; it's my life assignment. My clients depend on me to create spectacular spaces and environments that reflect their personal style. My purpose is to fulfill that by creating spaces where they can find peace, harmony, and comfort.

What is someone depending on you to fulfill? What's your divine assignment and life calling? What has God specifically placed you in this world to do?

Life is about listening to "your" heart, living in "your" truth, and pushing yourself to pursue your personal purpose. It's important to realize that the things that excite your soul aren't random. They are connected to your purpose. Strive after those things. In fact, I suggest you race toward them like your tail is on fire! If you don't, someone else will and you will ultimately have regrets.

Don't compromise your purpose and live a life of regrets. Go after your dreams! It's never too late to walk in your divine purpose.

Living purposefully is getting up, going out, and having the tenacity to make things happen. Passionately pursue your purpose with all your heart. To live purposefully, you must have a clear VISION. Visions usually start with the dreams, desires, and hopes of your heart, while using your God-given gifts and abilities inside of you.

Specify your vision through prayer, visualize it mentally, claim it through faith, and expect it through God's promise. Even if it seems far fetched, and larger than what you are currently capable of. Your vision should always exceed your ability. However, you can't leave out the work! Many dream and imagine, but FEW are disciplined enough to EXECUTE and finish!!

We must always stay positive and visualize our dreams like they've already come true. Keep your eyes on the prize and run to the finish line with all your heart! Don't dare think of anything opposite of what you're praying for. Believe and be consistent with hard work and the spirit of completion. Finish what you start!

Know that a dream without work will result in a nightmare of nothing. Stretch toward your potential. Don't give up. HOLD ON TO YOUR VISION, EVEN WHEN THE GOING GETS TOUGH! It's the key to unlocking your purpose.

> *Write down the message I am showing you in a vision. Write it clearly on the tablets you use.*

> *Then, a messenger can read it. The message I give you waits for the time I have appointed. It speaks about what is going to happen and all of it will come true. It might take a while but wait for it. You can be sure it will come. It will happen when I want it to.*
>
> ~ Habakkuk 2:2-3

Living purposefully will require living life with a priority perspective. This takes discipline. For most, living a lifestyle with discipline is easier said than done. It's hard work and we must hold ourselves accountable for our daily time management. We must hold ourselves accountable for our daily management. Those twenty-four hours need to be used wisely. I love the statement: *"We all have the same twenty-four hours as Beyoncé!"* In fact, the statement couldn't be more true. Take ownership of your time, prioritize your day, and be the superstar of your own life.

I recently spoke to a group of young ladies and told them if I could tell my younger self-anything, it would be not to waste time. We often tell our kids…" You have your whole life ahead of you." When in fact, we must tell them to value time and use it wisely.

"Time is like a river. You cannot touch the same water twice, because the flow that has passed will never pass again."

~ Author unknown

Discipline is major when living purposefully! Without discipline, your success will be tainted. Think of any superstar or athletic champion. They are not superstars by accident; they are game changers because of their discipline and hard work. Beyoncé and Steph Curry are legends because they use their 24 hours to the best of their ability to perfect their crafts.

You have to be disciplined enough to train like Beyoncé and Steph in order to gain the privilege of winning. If you want to win at the game of life, it will take discipline.

When living purposefully, there are so many areas in our life that need discipline.

"Productivity is never an accident. It is always the result of a commitment to excellence, intelligent planning, and focused effort."

~ Paul J. Meyer

Truth be told, I was once guilty of WASTING TIME. I'm honest enough with myself to acknowledge that I wasted valuable time making excuses! I should have made the time to make important life decisions as opposed to frivolous ones. Now that I'm older and wiser, I can encourage others to be cognizant of time. Want to go to college…enroll! Want a job…apply! Want the podcast…launch it!

STOP WASTING TIME!!!

When living purposefully, you can't be a procrastinator or an excuse maker. You must have discipline, dedication, passion, and a plan. There needs to be a firm focus on the desired goal and action to get there in order to live purposefully. You can't have a dream and not be prepared to put in the work.

POSITIVE · PASSIONATE · PURPOSEFUL

Living purposefully is a result of waking up daily, being intentional and productive. Even when some days are darker than others, finances are tight, or you're stressed and tossing and turning at night. This is not the time to entertain distractions, evaluate your life and determine what's not aligned with your purpose. Furthermore, be cognizant of what's wasting your time and make the necessary adjustments.

When you decide to walk in your purpose, it can often call for temporary isolation to really get in tune with yourself. This doesn't mean you will remain isolated forever, just until you get a grip on the things you truly want for your life.

As much as we like to be social and amongst friends, there's truly power in being alone. Consider it your "ME ZONE."

We must learn to tune out distractions and noise by listening to our own voices and soul. Sometimes you need to be the one giving yourself advice and trusting your instincts.

Deep down, your soul already knows what you need. We must take time to work on our substance by loving ourselves, respecting ourselves, healing ourselves, knowing ourselves, and more importantly correcting ourselves.

During this time, you must align your actions with your priorities. Dig deep within yourself and learn to focus and put in the work to make those dreams come true. This will take a huge level of sacrifice and dedication, which may result in you missing a few social events. Sundays are my absolute favorite days; however, I've missed several

Sunday fun days while being dedicated to getting this very book completed. You may even lose a few friends, miss some amazing engagements, and experience some weary days and restless nights. The people meant to be in your life will understand, support, and encourage you to pursue your dreams. They will be there to celebrate you walking in your purpose. Trust me, the sacrifice will be worth it in the end.

"Consistency is harder when you have no one clapping for you. You must clap for yourself during those times. You have to learn to be your biggest fan."

~ Arthur unknown

I witness so many people being distracted by what others are doing. It's a known fact that comparison is a thief of joy. It takes far too much time to constantly compare your life to someone else's. Use that time to focus on perfecting and performing your purpose.

Life is not a competition. I repeat. Life is not a competition! Your blessings have your name on them. If something is truly destined for you, it will come to you. You won't miss it. We all have a designated time to shine, which means, sometimes you have to wait a moment, for your moment. Be patient, be positive, keep grinding, and know your time is coming.

We should embrace and celebrate every season in our lives, hard times teach valuable lessons. More importantly, never hate during your wait! Never envy another person's life or success, nor should you discount where you currently are in life, as every season is important.

There's is no competition when you are authentically walking in your purpose.

~LaShonda Pierce

There are valuable lessons along the journey. Don't grow weary while waiting on your hard work to pay off, lay a brick every day toward living the life of your dreams. Hang in there and be encouraged and inspired by those in the position of life you admire. Emulate, congratulate, and keep walking in your purpose. My pastor reminds us that mature faith is when you can celebrate the goodness of what God is doing in someone else's life, and be confident that he will do the same for you. Be encouraged!!

The Power of Living Purposefully

Use your downtime to learn more, prepare, and perfect your skill. You should strengthen and develop your craft every chance you get. If you want to be the next DJ Khalid, then you should be in the studio producing hits every chance you get. If you want to be the next Oprah Winfrey, then do the work!! A wise person never stops learning.

People often doubt their ability to succeed and say things like, "the market is over-saturated". Claiming there's already enough attorneys, boutiques, writers, web designers, singers, makeup artist, food trucks etc. That's simply not true, do what you were born to do. Understand and identify your niche and what will set you apart.

We live in a **HUGE** world and serve a **BIG AND MIGHTY GOD** that has made room for us to all to succeed. He will honor the desires of our hearts. My purpose has nothing to do with the next individual, and neither does yours. Please don't waste time living a life of comparison and competition when pursuing your purpose.

Celebrate your uniqueness. That beautiful quality that sets you apart is vital when recognizing and walking in your purpose. Have you been to any major retailer lately? There are tons of brands in the world that sell the exact same product, and guess what; they aren't focused on the other brands!!! They are focused on their personal brands and so should you!!!

Pursue your purpose and
LET THE GAMES BEGIN...

Think of your life's personal purpose like the game of bowling. While bowling, we are each assigned a personal lane. You have your lane and your personal pins. Most venues allow you to highlight YOUR LANE with your team name. (Insert your Life Brand here.)

For instance, my lane would be named "LaPierce Design, or LaShonda Pierce." Stay in your lane focused on your purpose. The targeted pins ahead of you represent your individual dreams and goals. The ball represents you chasing and accomplishing those goals. The ball goes hard and fast as it races towards the pins at a speed like no other.

Win your game, in your lane, in your world, in your control, and on your grind. Don't look or concern yourself with any other lane other than your own. Knock down each pin in YOUR LIFE! Tune in, concentrate, and focus on YOUR pins, and you will hit a strike every time!

Your purpose will be an incredible alarm clock. It will get you up early in the morning and keep you working late at night. Being purposeful is the fulfillment of living out your dreams. While pursuing those dreams, it's important to be intentional.

Learn to focus on what's important by strategically planning and mapping out your journey. Manage your time wisely. Many times, we procrastinate waiting on the perfect opportunity to unleash our dreams, showcase our talent, or launch ourselves. However, IT'S WISE TO MAKE PROGRESS NOT PERFECTION THROUGH SMALL BUT CONSISTENT STEPS THAT WILL HELP YOU FULFILL YOUR PURPOSE. Life is short,

The Power of Living Purposefully

don't waste time looking for the perfect opportunity, have some courage and get out of your own way and live purposefully.

At the end of the day, life is about listening to your heart, living in *your* truth, and being unapologetic about pushing *yourself* to pursue *your* personal passions. Getting up working at something just to get by isn't nearly as fulfilling as doing what you truly love. I challenge you to stretch toward your potential. Don't give up. Hold on to your vision, It's the key to unlocking your purpose.

If you don't get up and go get it you'll never have it.

~LaShonda Pierce

Another important factor to living purposefully is identifying the "whys" in your life. This will help inspire you to walk vigorously toward a purposeful life. The why is typically a motivating factor to why you need to go hard, not quit, and push yourself to your greatest potential.

As adults, the most obvious and common reason "why" we get up every day and work our tails off is that we all have priorities and fiscal responsibilities! Paying bills monthly is a responsibility that has to be done. Let's think about the personal whys in our lives. Is it those beautiful kids, who look up to you that you need to provide, protect, and inspire to live their best lives? Perhaps, it's that naysayer that you'd like to prove wrong, or that family legacy you'd like to uphold. Whatever your why is, let it motivate you.

The Power of Living Purposefully

I challenge you to look in the mirror daily and know that your life has a specific purpose. Declare and decree your life by making the world feel your presence, your purpose and why you were created. Appreciate the talents that you have been blessed with and use them to take over the world!

We have to be in it to win it with no backing down or giving up. Be mindful that what you don't do, someone else will!! At the end of the day, when it's all said and done, I encourage you to diminish excuses and push yourself harder. Prove it to yourself!! Allow the days that you feel like giving up to energize you to push forward harder.

Here's what I want you to do daily…

1. Wake up each day with intention and a clear plan toward living a purposeful life. Make strides toward living your life to its fullest potential.
2. Starve your distractions and feed your focus.
3. Implement daily deadlines with determination.
4. Firmly focus on your goals for a greater impact on the end result of your life.
5. Focus on the dream that you want to fulfill and your why. Then, let that be the fuel to your fire.

PRAYER FOR PURPOSE

Heavenly Father, thank you for uniquely designing me with a talent and a purpose for my life. I humbly seek You today. Teach me how to take who I am and who I desire to be and use it for a purpose greater than myself. Help me acknowledge my true divine purpose. Use me, God, to honor my strengths, talents, and purpose to be a blessing to myself and others in the mighty name of Jesus.~ Amen

> *Many are the plans in a person's heart, but it is the Lord's purpose that prevails.*
>
> ~ Proverbs 19:21

POSITIVE · PASSIONATE · PURPOSEFUL

Ask yourself the following questions:

What is your true purpose and calling?

_____

_____

_____

List three words that specifically describe you.

_____

_____

_____

What priorities should you put first while pursuing your purpose?

_____

_____

_____

_____

What areas of your life need more discipline?

_____

_____

In what ways have you been stagnant and procrastinating for too long?

_____

_____

_____

Use the lines below to list your short- and long-term goals then make SMART goals of how you will achieve them.

_____

_____

_____

_____

_____

_____

YOU'LL BE JUDGED.

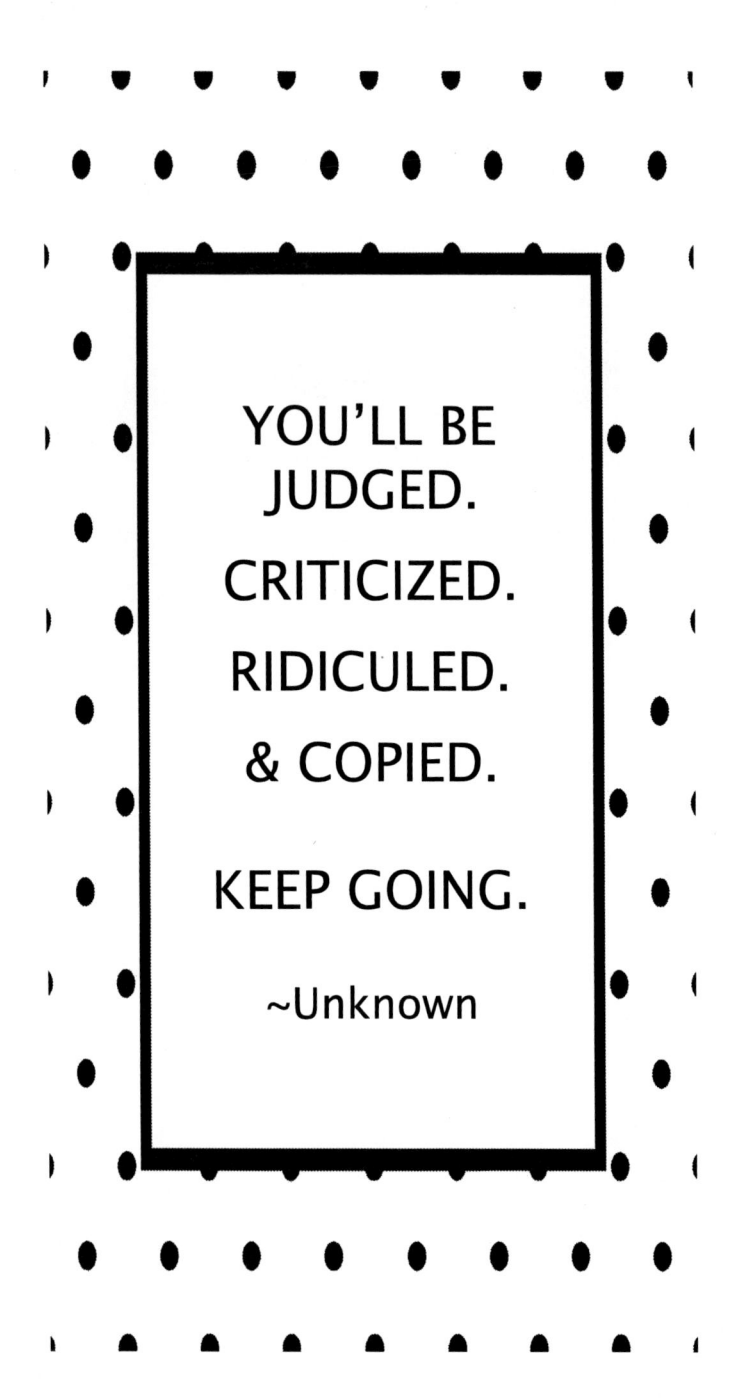

CRITICIZED.

RIDICULED.

& COPIED.

KEEP GOING.

~Unknown

WHEN IT'S ALL SAID AND DONE...

I hope that this book has been a blessing to you, by giving you insight on being positive, igniting your passion, and living purposefully.

I sincerely think you for supporting this book and the PPP lifestyle. I wish you unlimited peace, positivity, and an overflow of love.

If you're looking for me, I'll have my megaphone in hand making positivity louder every day. In my lane, living purposefully, sharing smiles, spreading love, dodging bad vibes and negativity!

Please put on your positive pants and join me on the journey of this lifestyle movement. Do it for the gram and stay connected with me via social media with the hashtag #positivepassionatepurposeful

Follow me on IG @ positivepassionatepurposeful

Email me at positivepassionatepurposeful@gmail.*com*

www.positivepassionateandpurposeful.com

Be positive, stay passionate and live purposefully!

THANK YOU

Thank you, Father -God for your unwavering hand in my life. Heartfelt thank you's to my friends and family for encouraging and cheering me on while writing this book.

Thank you Kristi Jackson, of the Women CEO project for pushing me to put my pen to the paper. Thank you to my pastor, Byron Stevenson, and friend, Irishea Hilliard, for your spiritual leadership and teaching.

Many thanks to my dear friends Charlie Rhodes and Tineal Sloan for always having a listening ear, and showering me with love and support during this entire process.

Krystyle Barrington, Robin Surface & Leah Pride I sincerely thank you for your time, talent and assistance. Finally, thanks to everyone who has added positive value in my life, I'm forever grateful.